CW00942281

THE ART OF BATMAN BEGINS

TITAN BOOKS
LONDON

THE ART OF BATMAN BEGINS

Shadows of the Dark Knight

BY MARK COTTA VAZ

Batman created by Bob Kane

THE ART OF BATMAN BEGINS

1 84576 094 8

Published by
Titan Books
A division of
Titan Publishing Group Ltd
144 Southwark St
London
SE1 0UP

Visit our website:
www.titanbooks.com

First edition June 2005
10 9 8 7 6 5 4 3 2 1

Designed by Mike Essl.
Design Assistance by Roy Rub.

A CIP catalogue record for this title is available from the British Library.

Printed in the United States of America.

Page 1—Concept art of Batman. Simon McGuire. Digital.

Page 2—Batcave model with Batmobile mockup and cut-out Batman to scale. Nathan Crowley.

Pages 4–5—The offices of Wayne Enterprises overlooking Gotham City. Andrew Williamson. Digital.

Pages 6–7—Batman's Utility Belt, pneumatic grappling gun, ammunition cartridges, and Mini-Mines.

Pages 8–9—Concept art of Batman descending in the Narrows. Dermot Power. Digital.

Above—14-inch scale model Batmobile created by Art Director Nathan Crowley.

Page 13—Cyberscan of actual Batsuit, front view. Digital.

*To the memories of Dick Sprang, Batman artist supreme, and Will Eisner,
whose "spirit" lives on.*

BEGINNING   14

BATMAN'S GARAGE   24

BATMOBILE   30

WELCOME TO GOTHAM   58

SECRET HISTORY   89

INSIDE ARKHAM   113

ACKNOWLEDGMENTS   139

BEGINNING

"Criminals are a superstitious, cowardly lot, so my disguise must be able to strike terror into their hearts. I must be a creature of the night, black, terrible . . . a . . . a . . ."

—Bruce Wayne, *pondering his crime-fighting future in* Detective Comics #33, *November 1939*

To a kid in 1939, hankering for a comic book and with a dime burning a hole in his pocket, the May issue of Detective Comics must have had the impact of a lightning bolt. That title had the usual crook brandishing a drawn gun on almost every cover, but the front of issue #27 showed something different and shocking—a masked man in a dark, skintight, seamless suit with a cowl and a Dracula-like black cape, swooping down by means of a thick rope gripped in his blue-gloved right hand, his left arm squeezed around the neck of a hoodlum. The composition—like a movie frame—had them suspended in space, high above city rooftops. Below the title was a simple blurb: "STARTING THIS ISSUE: THE AMAZING AND UNIQUE ADVENTURES OF *THE BATMAN!*"

The image promised a character with the perfect blend of grace and strength. The Batman's cape swept out like wings, but clearly he wasn't flying—else why swing on that silken cord? Perhaps he was mortal, not one of the godlike

super heroes who had been dominating the comic book universe since the previous year, when a rocket ship from the doomed planet Krypton brought Superman to Earth. But *what* a mortal, with the strength to hold his own weight and that of another full-grown man with one powerful arm! There was also the promise of mystery in the way the Batman's mask concealed his eyes. If eyes are windows into the soul, those opaque and phantomlike slits conveyed an aura of menace—and secrets.

"The Case of the Chemical Syndicate," that first tale in *Detective Comics #27*, laid the cornerstone of the legend. We meet mustached, silver-haired Police Commissioner Gordon, who doesn't suspect that his friend Bruce Wayne, a bored young socialite, is the Batman. The story reveals that the "mysterious and adventurous figure" is engaged in "a lone battle against the evil forces of society"—rather a heavy hobby for a "bored" high-society playboy.

The secret behind Wayne's one-man war on crime was unveiled in a two-page tale subsequently printed in both *Detective Comics #33* and *Batman #1*. It was primal stuff: A fifteen-year-old boy is walking home after a movie with his parents, Thomas and Martha Wayne. A gunman appears, demanding the lady's necklace. Her husband leaps to her defense and both are shot to death. The teary-eyed boy is suddenly alone in the street with their sprawled corpses. A few days later, at his bedside, the boy prays for vengeance and pledges to become a master scientist and attain physical perfection; after many years, his obsessive goal is achieved. Finally, we see the climactic scene of the brooding young man sitting alone in front of the fireplace on a moonlit night in the mansion inherited from his father, talking to himself. "I am ready, but first I must have a disguise," Bruce Wayne mutters when, like destiny incarnate, a bat flies in through an open window. The bat induces a vision, sealing Wayne's crime-fighting persona, and he embarks on his sworn path of revenge.

The whole thing took twelve bare-bones comics panels. But decades of artists and writers to come would revisit and elaborate upon that origin story and the legend that unfolded from it—a world created by Bob Kane, a twenty-four-year-old cartoonist who laid the groundwork with writer Bill Finger and a crew of unaccredited ghost artists, including Jerry Robinson and Dick Sprang.

Above—Detective Comics #27. Bob Kane. May 1939.

Opposite page—Detective Comics #33. Text by Bill Finger. Art by Bob Kane. November 1939.

Pages 14–15—Batman's debut in Detective Comics #27. Bob Kane. May 1939.

AS THE YEARS PASS BRUCE WAYNE PREPARES HIMSELF FOR HIS CAREER. HE BECOMES A MASTER SCIENTIST.

TRAINS HIS BODY TO PHYSICAL PERFECTION UNTIL HE IS ABLE TO PERFORM AMAZING ATHLETIC FEATS.

DAD'S ESTATE LEFT ME WEALTHY. I AM READY.. BUT FIRST I MUST HAVE A DISGUISE.

CRIMINALS ARE A SUPERSTITIOUS COWARDLY LOT, SO MY DISGUISE MUST BE ABLE TO STRIKE TERROR INTO THEIR HEARTS. I MUST BE A CREATURE OF THE NIGHT, BLACK, TERRIBLE...A..A...

..AS IF IN ANSWER, A HUGE BAT FLIES IN THE OPEN WINDOW!

A BAT! THAT'S IT! IT'S AN OMEN. I SHALL BECOME A BAT!

AND THUS IS BORN THIS WEIRD FIGURE OF THE DARK.. THIS AVENGER OF EVIL. "THE BATMAN"

It seems inevitable that the Batman mythology would be taken up by filmmakers, as it's perfect for the movies, both in its dramatic premise and atmospheric look. Batman's world is nocturnal, the chill of night often emphasized with waterfront fog or mists seemingly blown in by a cold wind from some damp moor. It is an urban world of silhouetted rooftops under Halloween harvest moons, black brick tenement walls swept by police spotlights, and shadowy streets, the stalking grounds of the underworld.

"Batman's world was more cinematic than Superman's," Jules Feiffer declared in his 1965 book, *The Great Comic Book Heroes*. Feiffer hailed Bob Kane's use of "angle shots" and his distinction as the only DC Comics artist "who managed to get that Warner Bros. fog-infested look." It was a prescient comment—Warner Bros. and DC Comics would eventually become divisions of the same media and entertainment conglomerate. In Batman's fiftieth-anniversary year, that synergy fueled director Tim Burton's *Batman*, a film for which production designer Anton Furst rendered one of the most memorable cityscapes in movie history, a gothic Gotham City that was a menacing reflection of its psychopathic criminal underworld.

Warner Bros. released four Batman movies in an eight-year span, the last being 1997's *Batman & Robin*. The character would remain alive and well in DC's serialized comics and graphic novels, and in animated productions and other media. But after that fourth live-action film, Batman disappeared from movie screens.

In *Batman Begins*, Batman has finally reappeared in the flesh. The title says it all—a return to the character's origins, and also a fresh start for the celebrated film franchise. Director Christopher Nolan, whose credits include *Memento* (2000) and *Insomnia* (2002), helmed the production, with actor Christian Bale suiting up as the Dark Knight. Bale was pictured on the cover of the June 2004 issue of *Entertainment Weekly*, gazing out intensely, shrouded by the shadow of Batman's famous cowl. He told the magazine he had been attracted to the project because of Nolan's involvement "and the knowledge that what was being aimed for was a reinvention of Batman lore."

Gotham harbor at night. Simon McGuire. Digital.

"After [*Insomnia*], I was looking to do something on a grand scale, a grand canvas," Nolan explained. "I wanted to do the kind of blockbuster entertainment I had enjoyed as a kid, something that creates an entire world and characters you invest in. One of those films I loved as a kid was *Superman* by [director] Richard Donner and Christopher Reeve, which made you *believe* in that character, in that story."

For Nolan, Batman was an obvious and time-tested subject for creating outsized adventure and conjuring a whole world. There was also, however, an unexplored aspect of the character that compelled him to summon Batman from the shadows and back to the big screen.

"Tim Burton's *Batman* is fascinating, but very stylized," Nolan mused. "Previous movie versions created a world so exotic that Batman naturally fit in. I felt there was this odd cinematic gap—no one had taken Batman on as a *realistic* character. Batman is, after all, a mortal guy. Even the Gotham of the comics, of all the comic locations, while certainly heightened and exaggerated, still reflects people's very real worries about their own society. What hadn't been done, for better or worse, was the notion of an extraordinary man in an ordinary world."

In Nolan's vision, *Batman Begins* would cut to the mythic heart of the character. There would be little touches embellishing or recasting the particulars for different nuances—it was decided it was an opera, not a movie, that the Waynes attended that fateful night, for example. But at the core level, Nolan and company were after a more far-reaching definition of Batman's origin, a greater context delineated by the elemental question: *What if Batman actually existed?* As they sought the answer, the ensuing revelations informed every aspect of the production. Their creative quest echoed the legend itself—the *why* of Bruce Wayne's crusade, the *how* of his one-man war.

Nolan, an English American who grew up in London and Chicago, was a five-year-old kid in London when he was introduced to Batman through the popular television series starring Adam West, which first aired in England in 1966. (His fondest childhood memories include the wonder of a Viewmaster with 3-D images of the *Batman* TV show.) The show is historically regarded as a kitschy bit of pop art and a colorful example of the ironic whimsy of "camp," but as a boy, Nolan didn't catch the campy quality—he was in the thrall of the show's "cool" factor. Even then, he remembers, he felt the presence of deeper currents, something compelling about the character that shone through.

Death of Bruce Wayne's parents. David James.

"Some people disown the TV show, but when you're five or six years old, it's pretty exciting," Nolan reflected. "But what spoke to me was, really, the fundamental quality of this elemental, archetypal character. It was the idea of a powerful individual who's powerful purely through his own self-discipline, rather than through some external force. It was very compelling, particularly the idea of the double life, the secret identity."

The fact that Batman could encompass both the gaudy goings-on of the pop TV show and the dark weirdness of a Tim Burton movie, that he could be both groovy and gothic, spoke to the character's inherent mythic strength, in Nolan's view. Although Nolan didn't point his production team to specific *Batman* comics imagery (except regarding the dynamic presentation of the Batman costume, which is discussed later), he studied Batman's comic book history and the "evolutionary process" of the character.

"We referenced the comics, but not in a literal sense," Nolan explained. "In the sixty-five-odd years of the character there are things that have stuck and things that have been tried that haven't stuck. What emerges are the major milestones, the basic story of Bruce Wayne's parents being shot by a mugger and Bruce surviving and being raised by Alfred."

While the setting was adapted to be more contemporary, these basic icons are still featured, notably the indispensable Batmobile; but from the start there was a resistance to a lot of extraneous gadgets, gizmos, and gimmicks. "Chris was pretty stubborn on this point—this is the *origin* story," explained *Batman Begins* production designer Nathan Crowley. "It wasn't about providing the opportunity to make more toys."

"For me," Nolan said, "the thing that became apparent was the dark literary roots of the character—there's a lot of Hamlet and the Count of Monte Cristo, these essential underpinnings. I believe that what has allowed Batman to sustain these different, even wild, interpretations is that he's simple, elemental."

This book presents pieces of the dreaming that conjured *Batman Begins*' epic world—artwork generated during preproduction, that gestational period of art making and design that occurs before principal photography begins. Concept, or inspirational, art undergoes its own journey, full of countless triumphs and missteps on the path from the realm of pure imagination to the real world of sets, props, and costumes— the nuts and bolts of the seamless whole moviegoers finally see on screen.

Costume based on a design by Lindy Hemming. Simon McGuire. Digital.

BATMAN'S GARAGE

Director Chris Nolan and his wife, Batman Begins producer Emma Thomas, share a house on a narrow, tree-shaded street whose horizon line includes a piece of the hillside upon which are staked the letters that spell "HOLLYWOOD." Down a short driveway is the garage.

It was there, in the summer of 2003, that the art and writing departments hammered out the look and story of Batman Begins. "It was heaven— three months to think about design," Nathan Crowley smiled in recollection while driving to the Nolan house late in 2004, remembering the creative retreat that would become known as "the Garage" to the production's insiders. "It was a rare opportunity to be alone with the director to basically just play, to make models."

If any Warner Bros. executives needed to see works-in-progress, they had to come to the Garage. It must have set neighbors to wondering, the black limos occasionally parked on the quiet, residential street. Little did they know a group of filmmakers were in their own personal Batcave, dreaming up a world.

Crowley recounted that in the Garage, thousands of dollars' worth of model hobby kits had been "kit-bashed" (the process by which elements of various model kits are amalgamated) while designing the Batmobile, and towering stacks of Photoshopped images had been designed and pinned up. The space had seen the creation of everything from the Batmobile to miniature mock-ups of Gotham City and the slum island known as the Narrows to a foam-sculpted interior view of the Batcave, revealing the old, sunken foundations of Wayne Manor.

"It was jam-packed in here," Crowley said, estimating the space at six hundred square feet. Now two cars were parked inside the small structure, alongside a washer and dryer. The cars filled the space where two tables had been set up for making models. The pinboards that once posted a stream of concept art imagery were still up, but bare. Crowley pointed to where the computer and printer had been, where he had kept his band saw, the spot for the drafting table where he'd worked out the Gotham City monorail system originally built, according to the movie's story, by Thomas Wayne.

There were only a few things remaining as evidence of those busy months. On a side-wall bookshelf was a plastic-wrapped model kit of a Lamborghini Countach, left over from kit-bashing. Crowley pulled down from the bookshelf a thick folder he had left behind when he departed for London to set up the official art department. He opened it and spread out Photoshop composite images, including a photo of the final-approval Batmobile model dropped into street-scene collages of New York skyscrapers and Tokyo freeways. There were photographic references of teeming slums, which inspired the claustrophobic look of the Narrows, and a Photoshop image for Nolan's idea to have a flock of bats coalescing in a twilight sky and forming the shape of the Bat-Signal.

Crowley paused at a turn in the corner of the garage; hanging from a peg on the wall was the gas mask Christopher Nolan wore when the glue fumes and sprays used in the model making got too strong. Crowley gestured toward a small adjacent office, locked and shuttered, where Nolan had spent countless hours sequestered with screenwriter David Goyer, working on the first draft of the story.

BATMOBILE

The Batmobile was Nolan's first design assignment for Crowley. The director wanted to move away from the sleek hot rods of the past to create a vehicle tough enough to withstand the mean streets of Gotham City. Nolan proposed a fusion of a Hummer and Lamborghini Countach, and emphasized that the design had to produce a final car capable of maneuvering at speeds of up to 100 miles per hour, without any camera trickery simulating high speed. In fact, the watchword for the entire film was to avoid computer-generated visual effects, building and staging as much as possible live and "in-camera." "We had to design this stuff to work," Crowley summed up.

The director gave Crowley his Batmobile assignment on a Thursday, and Crowley went off and purchased hobby model kits to kit-bash a unique hybrid car. Crowley built the first Batmobile prototype model at his home, working on his kitchen table. "I like to make models, particularly cars," Crowley explained. "I don't think an illustration of a car works for design. A car is going to be 3-D and has to work from every angle. When I was kit-bashing, I realized I couldn't just cut together Hummer and Lamborghini Countach hobby models. I needed a cockpit, so I pulled out a P-30 airplane model for the cockpit."

An early "kit-bashed" Batmobile assembled by Nathan Crowley.

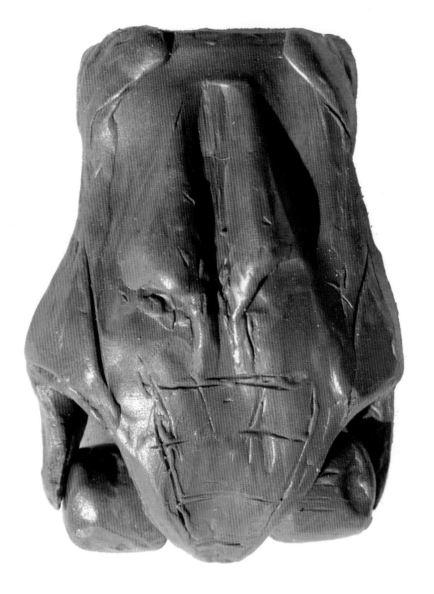

On the following Tuesday, Crowley returned to Nolan's house with the first kit-bashed Batmobile. That was when Crowley suggested to Nolan that he convert his garage into a preliminary art department to continue with the Batmobile work. The Garage art department kept rolling, and it was there that the entire scope of the production design was defined, establishing the look and laying the foundation for Batman's world.

The final *Batman Begins* Batmobile was parked at the Warner Bros. studio lot, overseen by transportation captain Dave Ragan. In the same lot was an object covered by a protective drape that could have been a mini-submarine. There was perhaps no better example of the differences between past *Batman* productions and the reinvention that Nolan and company were after than the sleek, thirty-three-foot-long Batmobile from *Batman & Robin,* the most recently released film in the franchise.

"This was the only car made for that movie," Ragan said, noting that because of its length and weight (more than 5,200 pounds), the car required a hydraulic system to get it off the ground. The thrust of the car's nose, which was fitted with a front spinning light to provide an oscillating effect, swooped back through a single cockpit to dual rear fins that were like the sharp edges of a windblown bat cape. The central flame exhaust, characteristic of past Batmobile designs, had been dropped in favor of six rear exhaust ports.

Crowley nodded approvingly. "It's of its time—surreal, bright, flashy," he said. "But for our film we wanted realism, that audiences feel Gotham City could exist as a real place."

Opposite page—Clay models created by Nathan Crowley.

Left—Model kit assembled by Nathan Crowley.

The *Batman Begins* car waited at the opposite end of the garage. This newest Batmobile was called "the Tumbler," a nickname coined during the top-secret design phase (the entire film was produced under the cover of a bogus production name, *The Intimidation Game*). The car looked perfect for an urban war zone: a black, fifteen-foot-long tanklike vehicle built low to the ground, complete with a rear exhaust port and a surface layered with aerodynamic flaps.

In the *Batman Begins* story, the Batmobile was built as a military "bridging vehicle" designed by the Applied Sciences Division of Wayne Industries and capable of short jumps at the push of a button. It's one of the cutting-edge military prototypes—along with a grappling gun and a soldier suit—that Bruce Wayne accesses with the help of Lucius Fox, a former Wayne Industries executive relegated to what has become a backwater division of the company.

Numerous versions of the Batmobile contributed to the illusion of the vehicle seen on screen in *Batman Begins*. There was a special model just for when Batman got into the car (in the film the car opens from the front end); a remote-control one-fifth-scale miniature for special-effects shots; a mock-up of the interior; and a full-scale car capable of being catapulted by air pressure for the vehicle's jump effect (perfect for bridging the chasm between the road and the entrance to the Batcave).

The Batmobile in the Warner Bros. garage was one of four stunt cars used in the film. First a Batmobile test car was made to check out everything from the mechanics to how the car handled at high speeds; four stunt cars, Tumbler numbers 2 through 5, were then built for the production.

"This is the best Batmobile yet," Ragan said, admiring the final result. He observed there was no front axle, with the front two tires built on a swing arm. The front tires were fat Hoosier brands designed for dirt-track racing, while in the rear were four huge Swamper tires, the ultimate off-roading wheels. Ragan opened the top (all stunt Batmobiles opened from the top) and dropped down into the tight cockpit—25 percent smaller than the mock-up used for interior views. The engine was flush to the back of the driver and passenger seats and was inscribed with a black bat logo and the label "Tumbler 005," marking it as the fifth car built. There were four propane tanks in the rear to fire up the exhaust-jet flame effect. The interior frame was a chrome molly steel roll cage straight out of NASCAR. On the driver's side door was a halon tank that at the push of a red button could suck out enough oxygen to snuff any life-threatening fires. Ragan switched on the ignition and the engine roared.

Top—The Wayne Enterprises military prototype vehicle upon which the Batmobile is based.

Above—Bridging the chasm to the secret entrance of the Batcave. David James.

Opposite page—The Batmobile bursts through the waterfall and into the Batcave. David James.

Pages 38–39—The Batmobile's computer status screens.

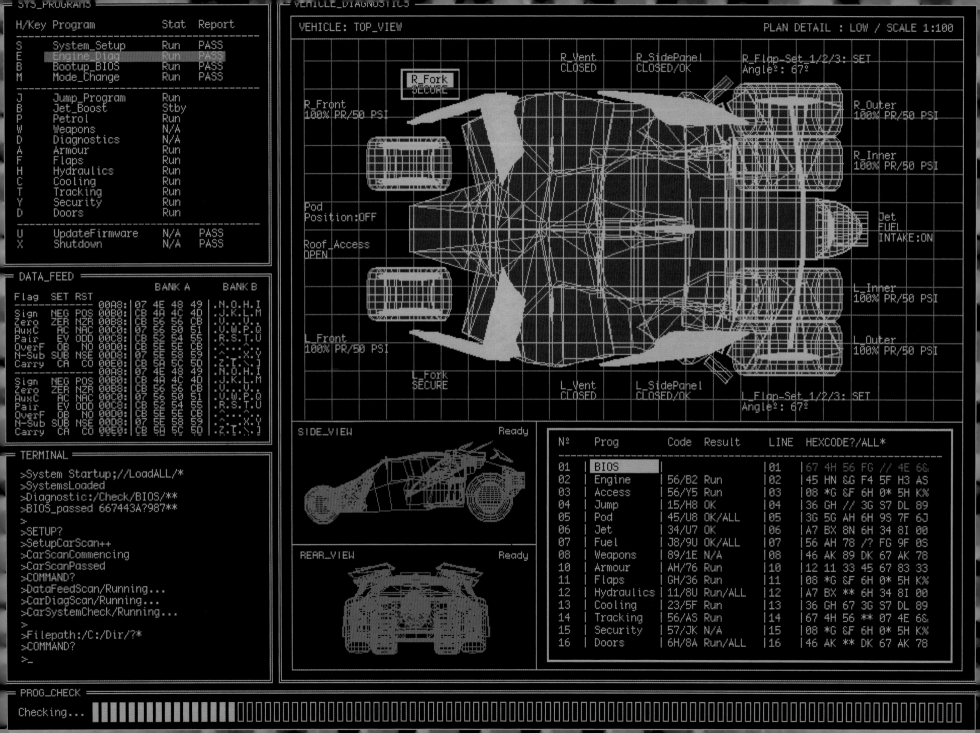

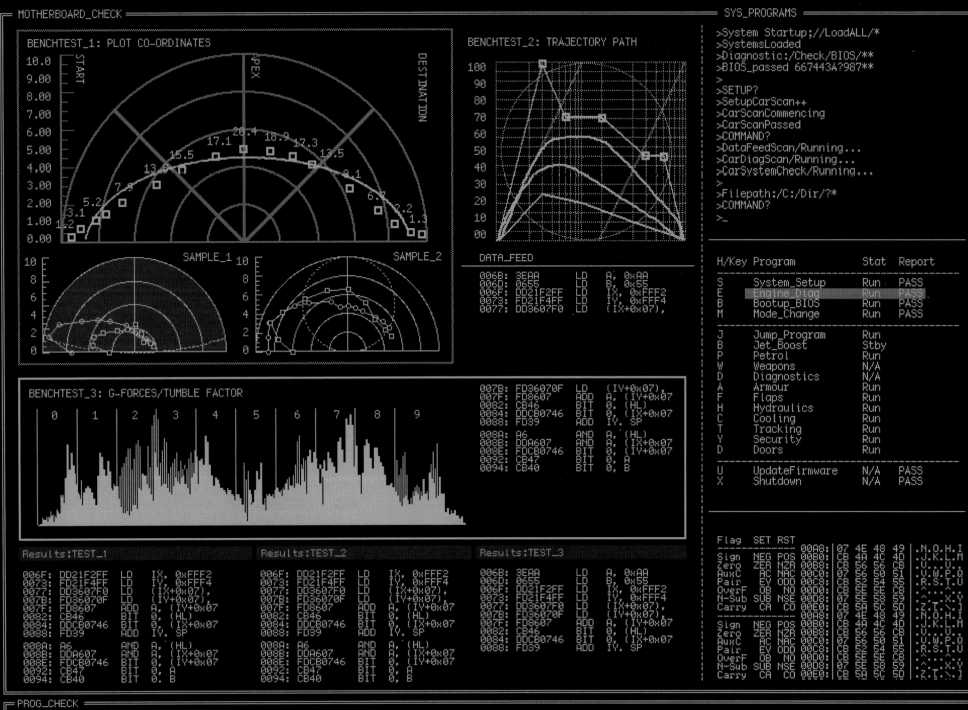

BATMOBILE

The design had indeed met Nolan's demands that the final car be able to function at high speeds. But despite being built Bat-tough, the vehicle's durability was still a concern to the production staff when the time came for a dangerous chase scene to be shot on cordoned-off streets in Chicago. In the end, all four stunt cars were used and came through without a scratch—except for one incident.

"One time, at 5:00 A.M., after we were done shooting, a police convoy was escorting the Batmobiles away when a drunk driver smashed into the side of one of them," Crowley said, adding that there were no injuries and only minor damage—the only lasting effect perhaps in the darkly humorous image of a suddenly sobered driver explaining to a judge how he'd just run into the Batmobile.

The Batmobile had been the filmmakers' vehicle for getting into Batman's world, an archetypal symbol representative of the entire production. They realized, for example, that Gotham City, like Batman's car, should be slightly fantastic, yet functional.

"I had a specific idea of the tone of the film I was trying to achieve," Nolan said. "I chose to do that by cracking the Batmobile, to see what this fabulous car would be like in real life, to make it special, yet credible. I felt if we could take on one of the key elements and discover the actual form of that element, it would represent the tone and kick off the whole design process."

Pages 40–41—Final Batmobile, front view. Hoosier tires designed for dirt-track racing ensure excellent traction. Absence of a front axle enables the Batmobile to make extremely tight turns. David James.

Pages 42–43—Final Batmobile, rear view. Four massive 44-inch Super Swamper tires flank an exhaust jet. The jet is a split-second after-burner utilized in car chases and adds thrust during rampless jumps. The Batmobile's jet wash is powerful enough to shatter the windshields of encroaching vehicles. David James.

Left—The final Batmobile. David James.

Pages 46–47—Rooftop getaway storyboards. Martin Asbury and James Cornish. Pencil and ink.

45

51.

A

BAT CAR
FLASHES
ACROSS
ROOF

CUT

BATCAR
L. to R
TO CAM.

B

COP
CARS B
RECEDE
IN B G

CUT

INSERT

BATMAN'S
FINGER
PRESSING
BUTTON

C

CUT

INSERT

REAR
SPOILER
FLIPS
UP ..

D

52.

C.U.
RACHE
SCREAM

A

CUT

MOVING
POV.
RUSHING
TOWARD
THE HOLE
IN THE
WALL.

CAM.

CUT

LOW ANG

THE BATC
SAILS
THRU' T
OPENING
INTO SPA

C

FLASH
CUT

BATMAN
AT THE
CONTROL

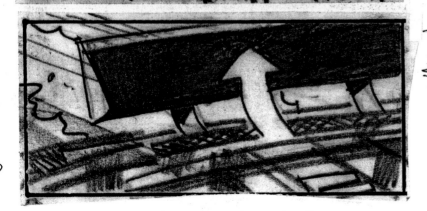

A

BATCAR
OVER
GAP
TO NEARBY
ROOF.

CUT

ANGLE
AS IT
CRASH
LANDS
AND..

B

CUT

WIDE
OF
ROOFTOP
.. IT
RACES
TO CAM.

C

CUT

" AND
FLIES
OFF
THE
END

D

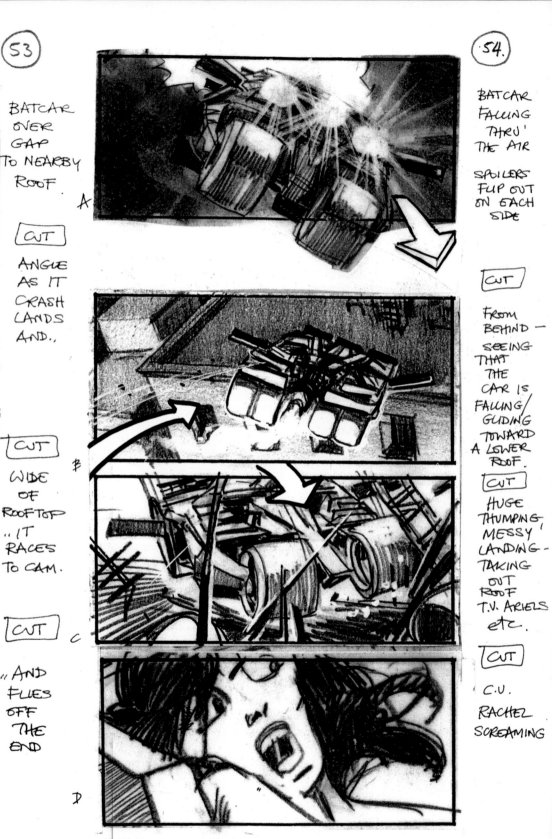

A

BATCAR
FALLING
THRU'
THE AIR

SPOILERS
FLIP OUT
ON EACH
SIDE

CUT

FROM
BEHIND —
SEEING
THAT
THE
CAR IS
FALLING/
GLIDING
TOWARD
A LOWER
ROOF.

CUT

HUGE
THUMPING
MESSY'
LANDING -
TAKING
OUT
ROOF
T.V. ARIELS
etc.

CUT

C.U.
RACHEL
SCREAMING

A

B

C

D

Opposite page and above—Batman evades the Gotham police in a high-speed chase. David James.

STEERING

Early designs included double joysticks as steering mechanisms for the Batmobile. More sensitive and quicker to respond to slight movements of the wrist, the joysticks could assist in high-speed, tight-quarters pursuits.

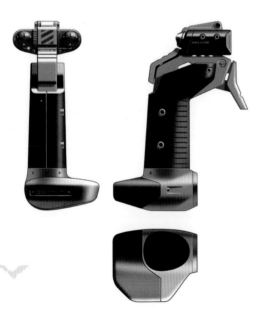

SEAT

Built of super-strong metal alloys and next-generation composites, the Batmobile's cockpit pod combines both ergonomics and safety. Ridden motorcycle-style, the floating gyroscopically balanced seat keeps Batman vertically inclined when the vehicle is at any angle.

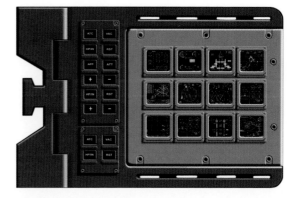

GENERAL DISPLAY

This multipurpose screen later became a rear-view video monitor that allows high-definition, multi-angle views of pursuers.

DISPLAYS

Design concepts initially placed numerous LCD screens within Batman's view. Later renditions utilized heads-up digital displays on ballistics-resistant windows for all electronics controls.

WEAPON DISPLAY

Used to control cannons in the Batmobile's nose, which fire standard ballistics as well as a variety of nonlethal rounds, including tear gas shells, fire-retardant gel canisters, and sticky foam.

MAPS AND GPS DISPLAY

A hard-wired Global Positioning System contains maps of Gotham City, including all street levels, alleyways, and thoroughfares, in addition to heights of buildings and depths of subterranean passages.

All illustrations by Dan Walker. Digital.

Interior concept of Batmobile. Dan Walker. Pencil sketch and digital.

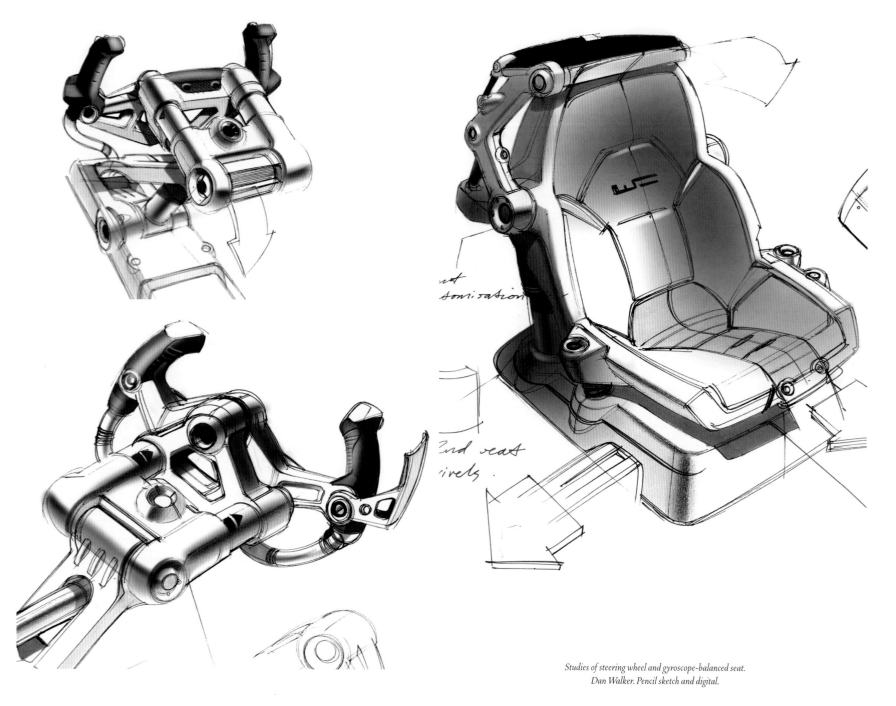

sonivation

2nd seat
swivels.

Studies of steering wheel and gyroscope-balanced seat.
Dan Walker. Pencil sketch and digital.

Cockpit with slight variation on the steering wheel design—a pointed shield is mounted on top.
Dan Walker. Pencil sketch and digital.

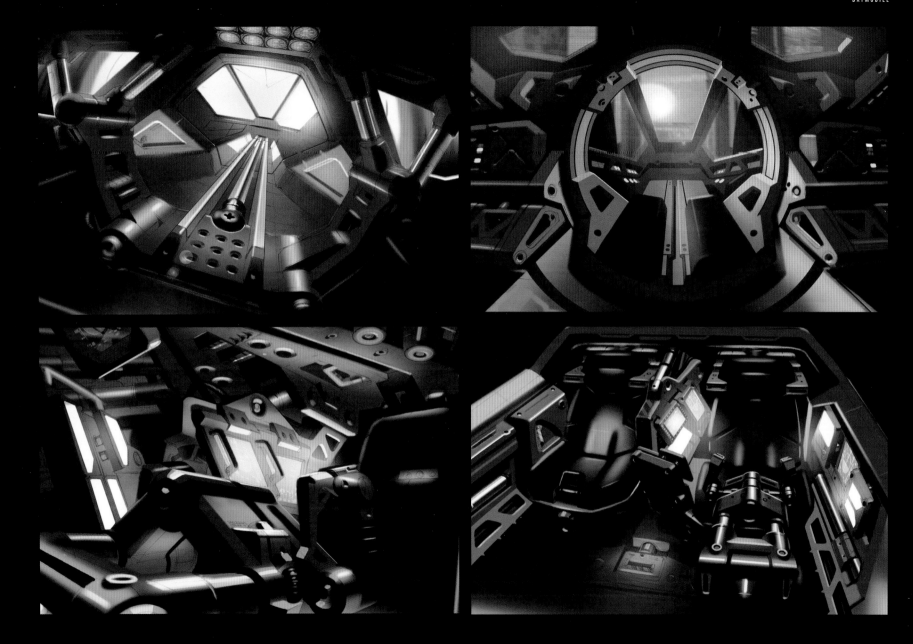

Above—Concept of Batmobile interior. Dan Walker. Pencil sketch and digital.

Opposite page—Sketch of Batman at the wheel. Dan Walker. Pencil sketch and digital.

WELCOME TO GOTHAM

"My standard definition of Gotham City is, it's New York below Fourteenth Street after eleven o'clock at night," veteran Batman comics editor Denny O'Neil once explained in the Batman history book Tales of the Dark Knight. *"Recognizably New York, but with emphasis on the grimmer aspects of the city."*

As with past Batman *movie productions, the Gotham of* Batman Begins *would be designed as a physical manifestation of the corruption in the city's soul; it would, however, be stripped of melodramatic, fantastical elements. Tokyo was a design influence, with Crowley pointing to a freeway in the middle of that city as typical of the haphazard urban planning familiar to any modern city dweller. Meanwhile, the geography and iconography of New York were primary inspirations, influencing the design of Gotham as a place of island boroughs. The final result was a modern metropolis with familiar evidence of urban disorder, heightened to an extreme: "Our Gotham City is New York on steroids," Christopher Nolan said.*

Again, it was the production's principle of realism that guided the evolution of the cityscape. "This is the great city in Batman's world, and it's not retro or futuristic—it's a city of today," Crowley noted. "We really wanted audiences to feel connected and familiar with the city. But then you have to figure out, how does a man who wears a rubber suit and drives a tanklike car fit in? There were a lot of issues." Crowley and Nolan agree that the Batmobile had unlocked the approach to the entire production. "While we were designing the car, we realized we couldn't design it without knowing what Gotham would look like," Crowley explained. In the symbiotic meeting of ideas, they realized that just as the Batmobile had to function as a real car, so too did Gotham demand its own inherent logic.

"Our Gotham was about commerce, not industry," Crowley explained. "Modern cities are commercial and not industrial. Gotham is a place of decay, but we didn't want to see smokestacks. We wanted the chaos of a city that has naturally grown to limits confined by water. We took New York as a footprint and imagined it in a chaotic state. It's hyperrealism, but with enough believability that you feel that Batman *could* live in our world."

"Batman, since he has no superpowers, deals with more real issues, which became important in both a design and narrative sense," Nolan added. "That allowed us to create a contemporary world so that the character could appear as extraordinary to the world of the film as he would in our world."

Key elements of Batman's city took form in Nolan's garage as he worked on the first draft of the script with David Goyer. At that early stage, when both story development and production design were emerging, the filmmakers embraced a conscious "parallel process," as Nolan called it. A vivid example of this synergy is found in Gotham's monorail transit system, which figures prominently in the storyline as having been designed by Thomas Wayne, and is also the setting for the climactic battle sequence. While the director and screenwriter were debating story points, the production designer was developing Gotham City Rail in the adjacent garage. That and other design projects enabled Nolan and Goyer to "deal with a real space, not an unimaginable space," Crowley noted.

Pages 58–59—Batman overlooks Gotham City. Dermot Power. Digital.

Pages 60–61—The Caped Crusader rests on a ledge overlooking the Narrows. Dermot Power. Digital.

Right—Gotham City Map. Mary-Ann MacKenzie. Digital.

Opposite page—Model of Gotham City, viewed from the north. Kate Grimble and Anna Bregman.

Above—Concept art of Gotham City girder bridge. Cyrille Nomberg. Digital.

Right—Concept art of Gotham cityscape. Cyrille Nomberg. Digital.

Opposite page—Art Director Nathan Crowley and Director Christopher Nolan building a monorail model.

"We didn't want to write a story and then come up with a look to match it," Nolan added. "We weren't imposing a specific style. I hope that the narrative and visual style is inextricably linked. That link very much goes back to the Garage.

"One of the things important to [cinematographer] Wally Pfister's photography and Nathan's design work was that to create an epic, we wanted to embrace different worlds and different locations. So the look of the film is extremely varied. We didn't want to be in one little area of Gotham, so there's a mix of old and new architecture. Then we're on a mountainside in Bhutan. We wanted to create a variety of textures to reflect the scale and grandeur of the wonderful old blockbuster entertainments that took you into a different world and around the world, things like *Raiders of the Lost Ark* and the best James Bond films, such as *Goldfinger* and *The Spy Who Loved Me*."

One of the environments Nolan wanted to see in Gotham was "a terrible slum," a crime-ridden district, known as the Narrows, so dangerous that even the police refuse to venture in. Crowley worked up the design in the Garage, drawing on stacks of references, including images of the shanty town of Kowloon, outside Hong Kong, which was demolished in 1994. Another inspiration was New York's Roosevelt Island, a strip of land in the East River that included the crumbling remains of a pre–Civil War smallpox hospital. In the end, the Narrows embraced the notion of a slum island, a seething maze of congestion and dark alleyways. This would also be the address of Arkham Asylum, the high-security lockup for Gotham's criminally insane villains.

Ultimately, the main Gotham island was imagined as three times the size of Manhattan. Wayne Plaza, in midtown, is the Gotham version of Wall Street, home to the corporate headquarters of Wayne Industries and a hub of the railway system.

Opposite page and left—Gotham City Narrows. David James.

Pages 68–69—An elevated monorail train flies over traffic in midtown. Andrew Williamson. Digital.

Pages 70–71—Storyboards of a duel between Batman and Rā's al Ghūl onboard the Gotham City Rail.
Martin Asbury and James Cornish. Pencil and ink.

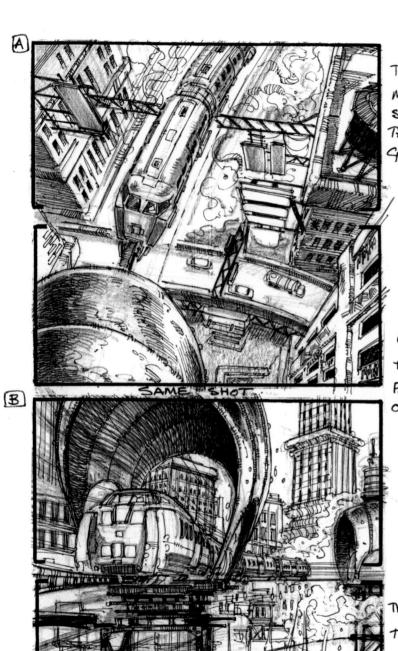

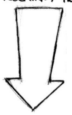

TOP SHOT AS THE MONORAIL STREAKS THROUGH THE CANYONS OF GOTHAM CITY.

CRANE DOWN TILT UP TO KEEP PACE WITH ON RUSHING TRAIN.

TRAIN BLASTS TOWARD CAMERA.

REVEALING THE BUILDINGS OF GOTHAM SLOWLY BEING ENVELOPED BY CRAWLING CLOUD OF FOG.

SAME SHOT.

CONTINUE TO CRANE DOWN PAN LEFT AS TRAIN RACES PAST CAMERA.

CAMERA BECOMES CLOAKED IN FOG.

CUT TO

RA'S LUNGES SWINGING HIS SWORD.

BATMAN PARRIES WITH HIS GAUNTLET SPARKS FLY FROM THE METAL SCALLOPS.

CUT TO

DOWN ANGLE. CONTROL ROOM.

TECHNICIAN WATCHES INSTRUMENTS DIALS ETC.

REACTION AS...

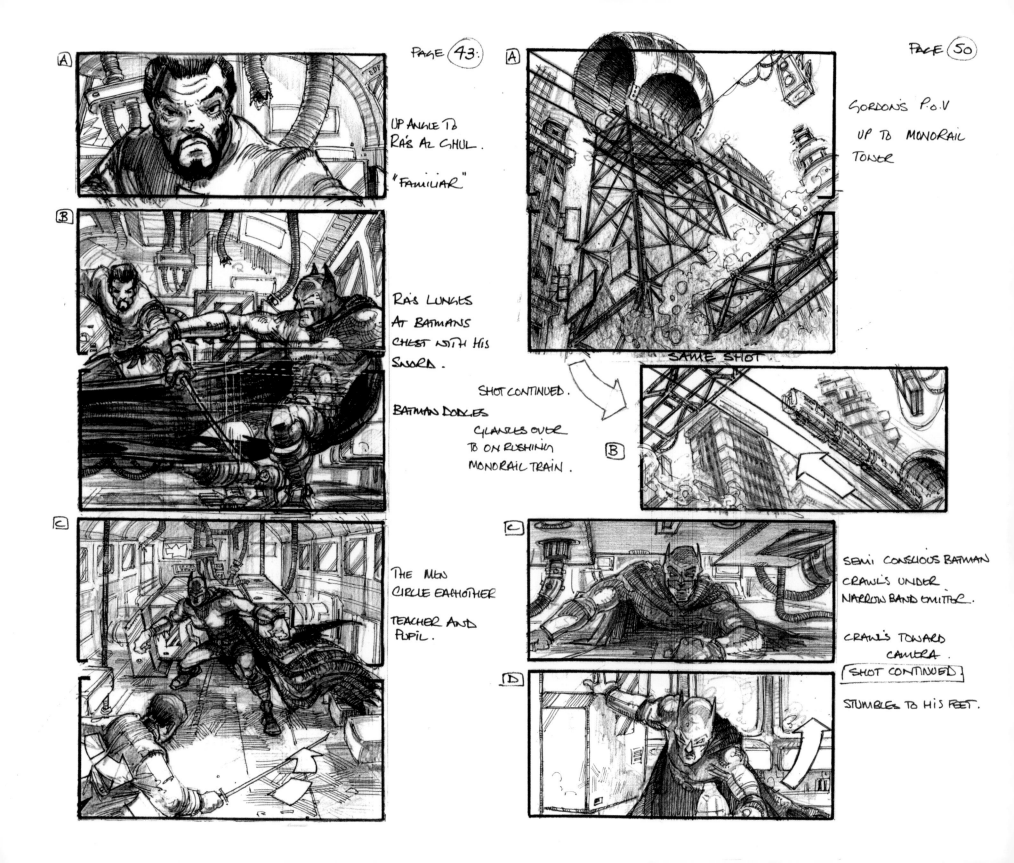

A

UP ANGLE TO
RA'S AL GHUL.

"FAMILIAR"

B

RA'S LUNGES
AT BATMAN'S
CHEST WITH HIS
SWORD.

SHOT CONTINUED.

BATMAN DODGES
GLANCES OVER
TO ON RUSHING
MONORAIL TRAIN.

C

THE MEN
CIRCLE EACHOTHER

TEACHER AND
PUPIL.

A

GORDON'S P.O.V

UP TO MONORAIL
TOWER

SAME SHOT

B

C

SEMI CONSCIOUS BATMAN
CRAWLS UNDER
NARROW BAND EMITTER.

CRAWLS TOWARD
CAMERA.

SHOT CONTINUED

D

STUMBLES TO HIS FEET.

Above—Train interiors and inter-train door system. Cyrille Nomberg. Digital.

Opposite page—Train interior study of angled track. Cyrille Nomberg. Digital.

Pages 76–77—Gotham at dusk; ever-present elevated train tracks crisscross the city. Dermot Power. Digital.

The filmmakers' realistic approach to developing Gotham extended to that other prominent piece of geography in Batman's world, the outlying countryside where Wayne Manor and the subterranean Batcave are located. The filmmakers, focused on their real-world concept, were concerned about the tons of concrete and retrofitting that would have been necessary if Bruce Wayne had actually remodeled the cavern underneath his mansion into the typically high-tech Batcave. Certainly Wayne could afford it—the comics had long ago graduated him from mere millionaire and trust-fund kid to billionaire head of a flourishing family corporation—but how could the necessary contractors and construction crews have done the job without raising questions?

The production followed the logical thread of the "New York model," as Crowley called it. If Gotham was New York and Wayne Manor an old family seat, then Connecticut was the appropriate inspiration for the ancestral home. Crowley spent hours wandering the Hudson River and exploring the rugged rock formations of the Palisades along its shores—these inspired the idea of a cave underneath the foundations of Wayne Manor that Bruce Wayne keeps in its natural state, a dank and dark subterranean lair for the Batman.

The secret entrance to the Batcave, cleverly concealed behind a thundering waterfall. David James.

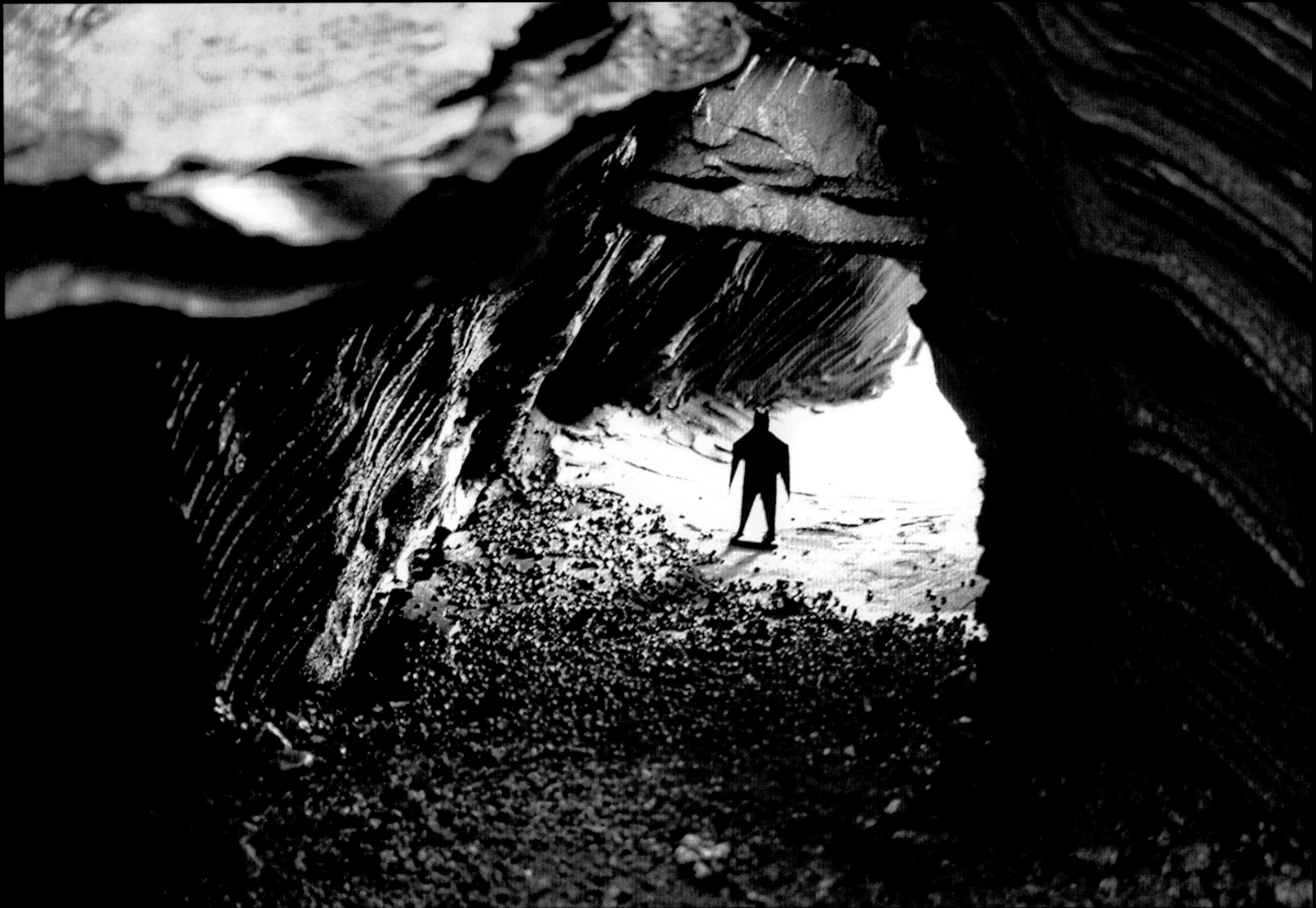

Above—Simple lights strung across empty expanses of the model Batcave.
Cutout Batman and Batmobile mockup to scale. Nathan Crowley.

Opposite page—Batcave model with a cardboard Batman to scale. Nathan Crowley.

SECRET HISTORY

In the original Batman story, it's a clear-cut path from young Bruce's vow of vengeance to that defining moment when a black bat inspires him to become a "weird figure of the dark." The intervening years of physical preparation are symbolized in one panel with Wayne single-handedly thrusting a barbell overhead. But in the minds of the Batman Begins team, there had to have been more intensive training, given the physical endurance Batman requires to make his nightly patrols, the iron constitution he needs to withstand cold and wicked weather, the mettle he must have to engage in hand-to-hand combat.

There is also a side of Batman that, however mortal he may be, has always bordered on the supernatural. Commissioner Jim Gordon often experienced this eerie aspect during the nights he waited on the rooftop where the Bat-Signal shone its beacon summoning the Dark Knight. Gordon would turn around and there they would be: two phantom eyes hovering in the dark. Then the tall figure would silently step out of the shadows and into the circle of the Bat-Signal's light. Batman's spooky appearances and disappearances always gave Gordon a start.

Above—Bruce Wayne trains in Bhutan; returning home to Wayne Manor,
he enlists the help of weapons expert Lucius Fox. David James.

Pages 88–89—Concept art of Falcone's body splayed across a spotlight,
creating an impromptu Bat-Signal. Simon McGuire. Digital.

DESIGN: LINDY HEMMING

DESIGN: LINDY HEMMING

DESIGN: LINDY HEMMING

Above—Character studies of Bruce Wayne the world traveler,
based on costume designs by Lindy Hemming. Simon McGuire. Digital.

The explanation that was developed in the Garage's writing department for Bruce Wayne's mysterious skills in stealth and superior fighting form took him to the Himalayas, a place never before associated with Batman's beginnings. The celebrated crime fighter the Shadow, the classic avenger from the days of radio adventures and pulp thrillers and a precursor to Batman, had once come here to learn the power of clouding men's minds. In *Batman Begins*, this is where Bruce Wayne forges his body and spirit into super crime-fighting form.

"Basically, the mythology of the comics suggests that Bruce Wayne leaves Gotham for seven years and travels the world," Nolan mused. "He consorts with criminals and learns their ways; he learns skills and improves his physical and mental abilities."

In the film, we witness the restless young man in trouble, confined in a dirty jail in Bhutan. He's emotionally scarred, a lost soul drifting aimlessly, with no interest in managing the family fortune and a washout at all of the prestigious schools his name and money had gotten him into. In prison, Wayne meets Ducard (Liam Neeson), mysterious agent of the sinister Rā's al Ghūl (Ken Watanabe), one of the most exotic villains from the Batman comics. In the comics al Ghūl was a tall, dashing figure dedicated to purifying the planet of humanity, a terrorist visionary drawn to desolate places and armed with the money, men, and weaponry needed to carry out his twisted campaigns.

Ducard reveals to Wayne the secret of al Ghūl's League of Shadows, which is headquartered in a fortified monastery in the Himalayas. It's a rite of passage just suffering through the physical hardship of getting to the remote monastery, but Wayne makes his way there to join Rā's al Ghūl's inner sanctum. It is here that Wayne finally confronts and steels himself against his greatest opponent—Death. He is taught the ninja techniques of shadowy stealth, the art of hand-to-hand combat, the secrets of using explosive powders, and mastery of weaponry. Most of all, it is during his rigorous training that Bruce Wayne learns how to be more than a man in the minds of his opponents—how to instill fear in his enemies.

Top—Elaborate scale model of Rā's al Ghūl's secret monastery. Cutting Edge.

Above—Constructing the façade in Iceland.

Opposite page—Bruce Wayne struggles through the snow to the isolated monastery; authentic Tibetan prayer flags hang from the eaves. David James.

Pages 94–95—Storyboards of Bruce Wayne's trek to the mountaintop. Martin Asbury and James Cornish. Pencil and ink.

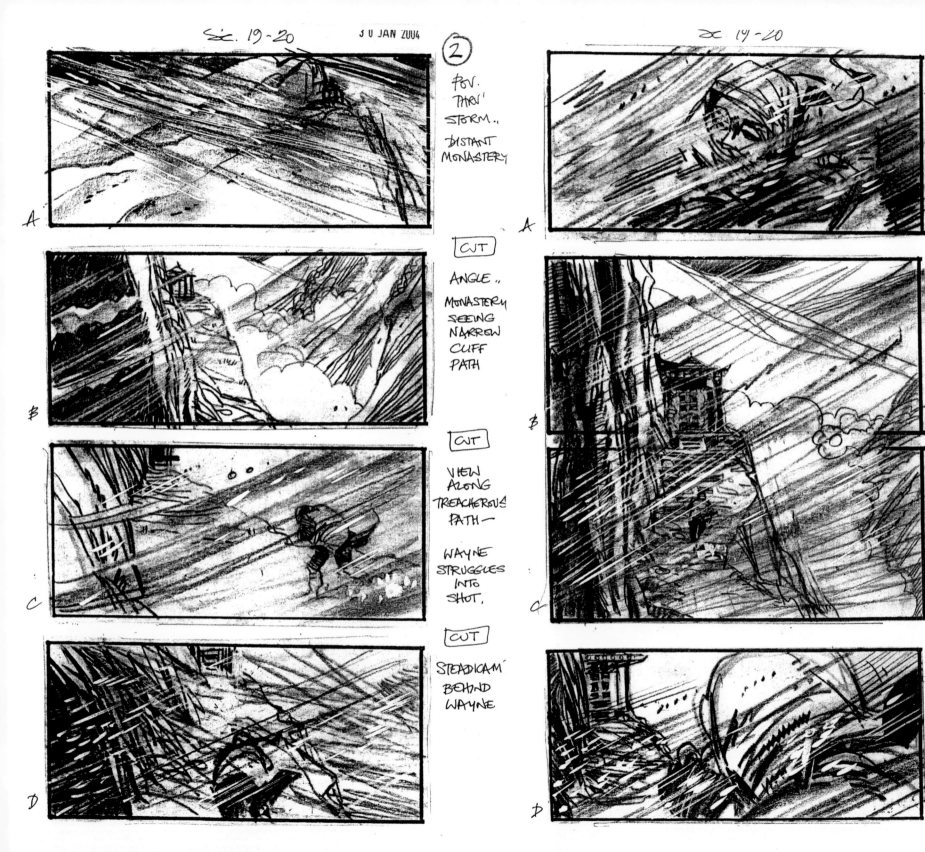

POV.
THRU'
STORM..
DISTANT
MONASTERY

A

CUT

ANGLE..
MONASTERY
SEEING
NARROW
CLIFF
PATH

B

CUT

VIEW
ALONG
TREACHEROUS
PATH —

WAYNE
STRUGGLES
INTO
SHOT.

C

CUT

STEADICAM'
BEHIND
WAYNE

D

CAM.
MOVES
WITH
WAYNE
BUNDLED
UP AGAINST
BLIZZARD

A

CUT

TILT
DOWN
↓

FROM
MONASTERY
TO
FIND
WAYNE.

B

CUT

MOVING
BEHIND
F.G.
WAYNE
TO
MONASTERY
ENTRANCE

D

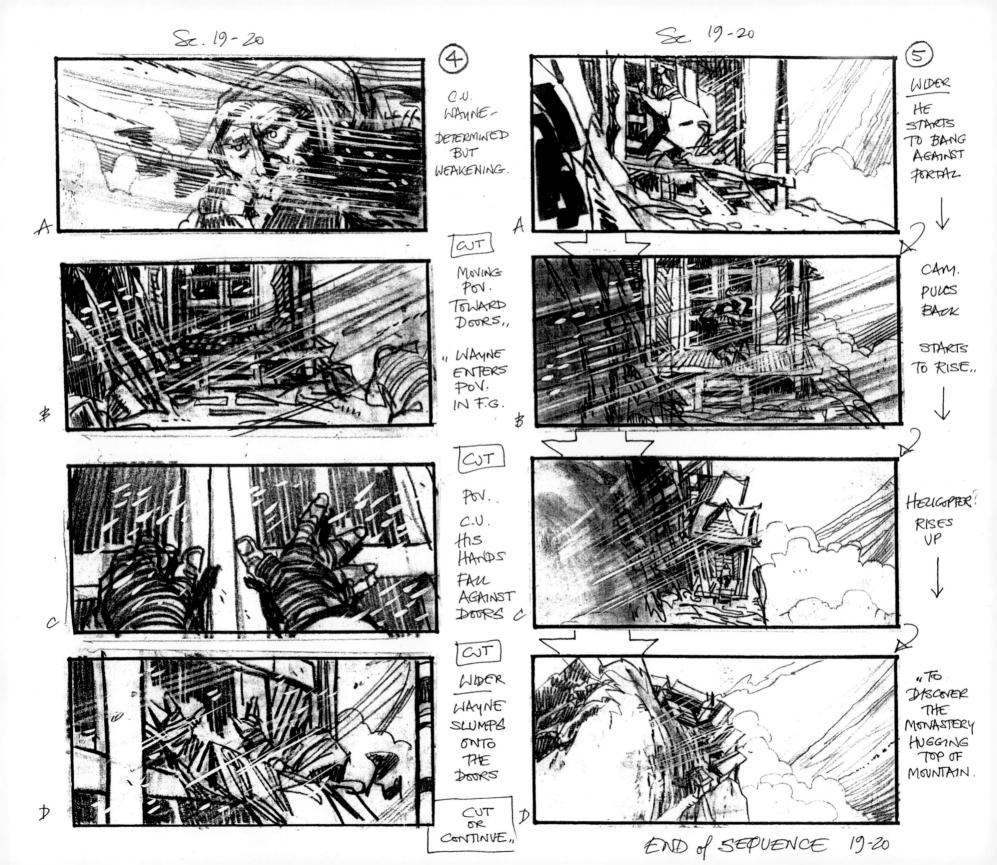

④

C.U.
WAYNE—
DETERMINED
BUT
WEAKENING.

A

CUT

MOVING
POV.
TOWARD
DOORS,,

"WAYNE
ENTERS
POV.
IN F.G.

B

CUT

POV.
C.U.
HIS
HANDS
FALL
AGAINST
DOORS

C

CUT

WIDER
WAYNE
SLUMPS
ONTO
THE
DOORS

D

CUT
OR
CONTINUE,,

⑤

WIDER
HE
STARTS
TO BANG
AGAINST
PORTAL

↓

CAM.
PULLS
BACK

STARTS
TO RISE,,

↓

HELICOPTER
RISES
UP

↓

"TO
DISCOVER
THE
MONASTERY
HUGGING
TOP OF
MOUNTAIN.

END OF SEQUENCE 19-20

For this Himalayan setting, the production wanted to use real locations, not to simply simulate a mountainous region on a soundstage or with computer-generated matte paintings. Location scouts chose a spot on the eastern side of Iceland, at a low enough elevation to avoid the risk of getting snowed in. Both the front doors of Rā's al Ghūl's mountaintop monastery and a complete village below were constructed at the location. For establishing shots of the monastery and village, a scale miniature set was built, while monastery interiors were constructed on soundstage sets at the Shepperton Studios in England.

The Iceland location provided its own fantastical world, including a frozen lake upon which a fight scene was staged. The village set itself was built near a glacier, which creaked as it crept forward as much as four feet a day.

"For the village, the main part was finding the right location," Crowley explained. "I could stand at the location and hammer down markers to find the shapes of buildings and lay it out. The location itself established the shape of the village, but it needed to ramble. There had to be a randomness, as if it had developed over hundreds of years."

When Bruce Wayne learns he has been trained by Rā's al Ghūl only to help the League of Shadows destroy what it saw as humankind's corrupt, decaying cities—beginning with Gotham—he violently breaks with the League. He escapes and returns home to assume his rightful place as master of Wayne Manor. Ahead of him lies a power struggle for control of Wayne Industries and the beginning of his secret crime-fighting crusade.

Above—Rā's al Ghūl in action pose. Simon McGuire. Digital.

Left—Bruce Wayne in training with the League of Shadows. David James.

Pages 98–99—Bruce Wayne breaks with the League of Shadows in a violent storyboard battle. Martin Asbury and James Cornish. Pencil and ink.

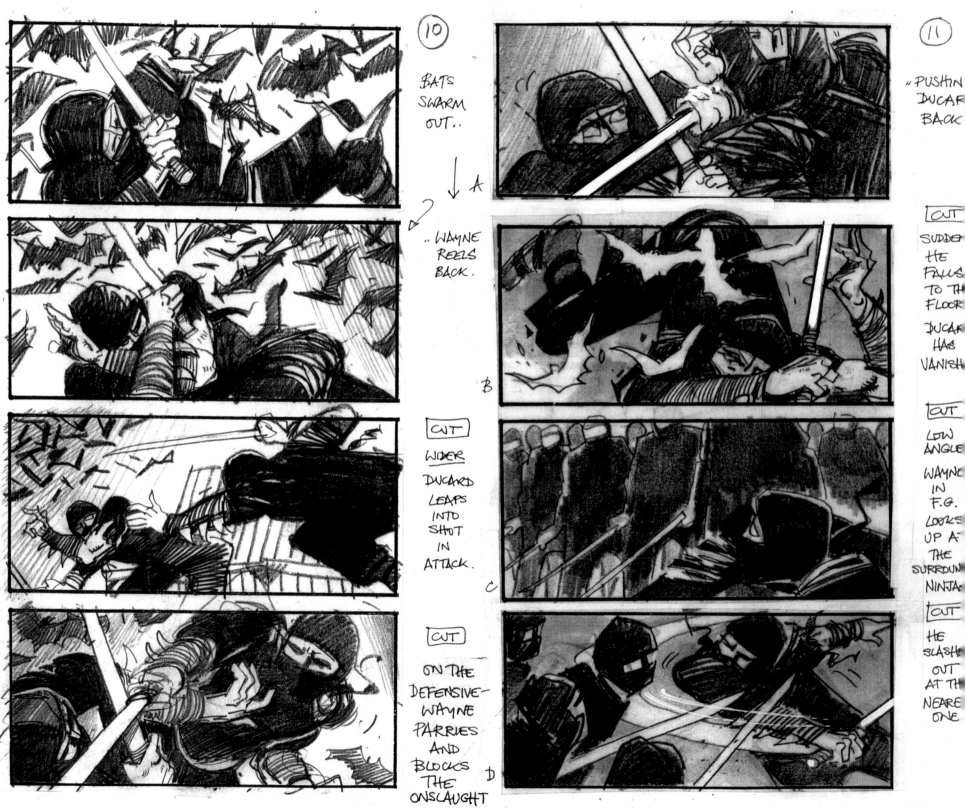

10

BATS
SWARM
OUT..

↓ A

.. WAYNE
REELS
BACK.

B

CUT
WIDER
DUCARD
LEAPS
INTO
SHOT
IN
ATTACK.

C

CUT
ON THE
DEFENSIVE-
WAYNE
PARRIES
AND
BLOCKS
THE
ONSLAUGHT

D

11

"PUSHIN
DUCAR
BACK

CUT
SUDDE
HE
FALLS
TO TH
FLOOR

DUCAR
HAS
VANISH

CUT
LOW
ANGLE

WAYNE
IN
F.G.

LOOKS
UP A
THE
SURROUN
NINJA-

CUT
HE
SLASH
OUT
AT TH
NEARE
ONE

(12)

A

C.U.
WAYNE
TURNS
TO
CAM.

[CUT]

(13)

A

DUCARD
GRABS
WAYNE —
SWORD TO
HIS THROAT

[CUT]

B

ANGLE
WE
SEE
LEGS
OF A
NINJA
[DUCARD]
ADVANCING
THRU' THE
RANKS.

B

[CUT]

B

C.U.
DUCARD
ANOTHER
SWORD
ENTERS
SHOT

CAM.
MOVES
BACK

C

OPTIONAL
WIDE

SEE
DUCARD
CLOSING
WITH
WAYNE

[CUT]

C

SWORD
PUSHES,
DUCARD'S
MASK
DOWN

CAM.
CONTINUES
MOVING
BACK

↓

D

CLOSER
OF
THE
SAME.

D

".. TO
DISCOVER
THAT
IT IS
WAYNE
WIELDING
THE
SWORD

HENRI DUCARD

Character sketches of Ducard. Simon McGuire. Digital.
Ducard appears in various guises throughout the film; his wardrobe can be elegant,
functional, or militant.

RĀ'S AL GHŪL

Character sketches of Rā's al Ghūl. Simon McGuire. Digital.
Al Ghūl's commanding presence is accentuated by flowing robes,
wickedly sharp gloves, and menacing postures.

LEAGUE OF SHADOWS

Character sketches of League of Shadows warriors. Simon McGuire. Digital.
Warriors carry weapons according to their needs and environment;
they are equally dangerous with a blade or a submachine gun.

Although half of Wayne Manor was created on soundstage sets, the production managed to shoot 50 percent of the manor scenes using both the exterior and interiors of Mentmore House, a storied estate in New York once occupied by the Rothschild family.

The icy landscape of Rā's al Ghūl's refuge is echoed in the Wayne Manor of *Batman Begins*, with its halls and walls of white plaster and marble and furniture wrapped like corpses in dust sheets. It is a house haunted by tragedy, with only loyal Alfred, the butler (Michael Caine), patiently awaiting the prodigal son's return.

"When Bruce Wayne leaves the monastery and comes home, we didn't want the feeling of this warm, wood-paneled place that has been the traditional picture of Wayne Manor, the kind of place where you'd expect he'd be met at the door by the butler and a serving tray with a glass of sherry," Crowley explained. "Instead, he returns to this packed-up house where everything is covered in whole dust cloths, where the marble makes it feel like a mausoleum—you feel the sadness. From a design standpoint, this was another place I didn't need to have illustrated; it was a place driven by a location scout."

Pages 102–103—Bruce Wayne and Rā's al Ghūl duel before Wayne is able to escape the monastery. David James

Top—An empty Wayne Manor outside of Gotham City awaits the return of young Bruce Wayne. David James.

Above—Bruce reflects on the past in the Wayne Manor greenhouse. David James.

Opposite page—Reliable Alfred welcomes Bruce back home. David James.

Pages 106–107—Elevation of Wayne Manor. Exteriors of Bruce's home in Batman Begins *were shot at the same mansion seen in Robert Altman's* Gosford Park*. Toby Britton.*

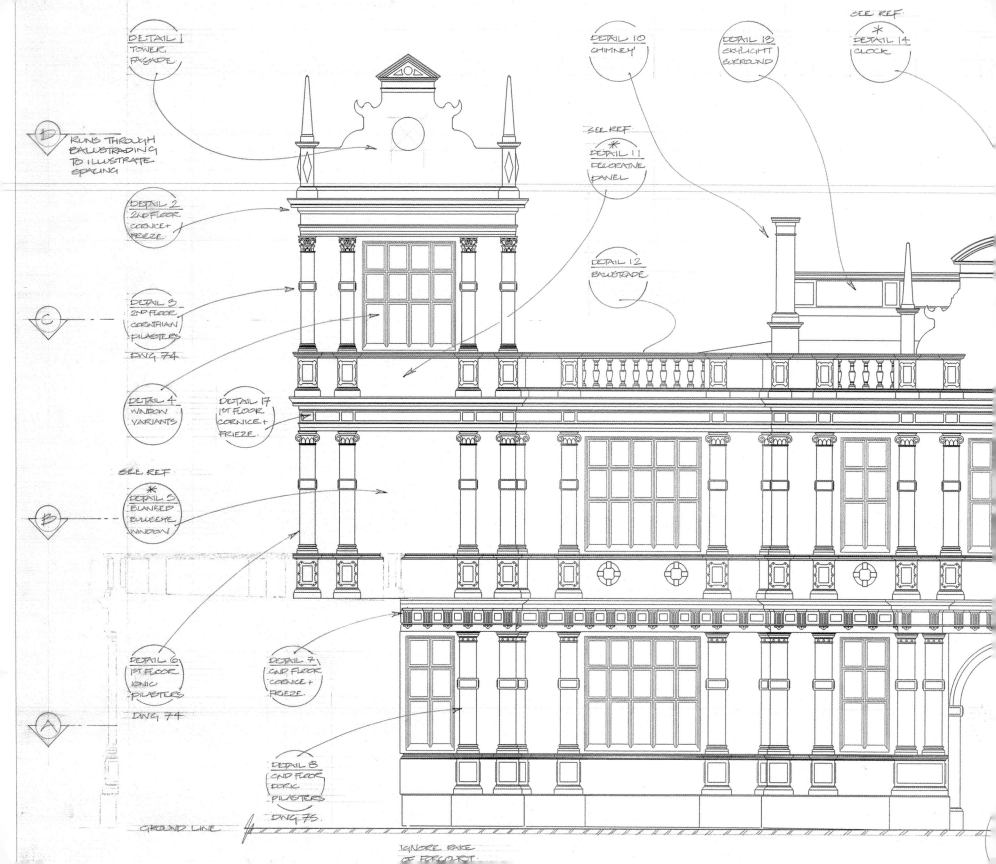

DETAIL 1
TOWER
FAÇADE

DETAIL 10
CHIMNEY

DETAIL 13
SKYLIGHT
SURROUND

SEE REF
*
DETAIL 14
CLOCK

D
RUNS THROUGH
BALUSTRADING
TO ILLUSTRATE
SPACING

SEE REF
*
DETAIL 11
DECORATIVE
PANEL

DETAIL 2
2ND FLOOR
CORNICE +
FRIEZE.

DETAIL 12
BALUSTRADE

DETAIL 3
2ND FLOOR
CORINTHIAN
PILASTERS
DWG 74

C

DETAIL 4
WINDOW
VARIANTS

DETAIL 17
1ST FLOOR
CORNICE +
FRIEZE.

SEE REF
*
DETAIL 5
BLANKED
BULLSEYE
WINDOW

B

DETAIL 6
1ST FLOOR
IONIC
PILASTERS
DWG 74

DETAIL 7
GND FLOOR
CORNICE +
FRIEZE.

A

DETAIL 8
GND FLOOR
DORIC
PILASTERS
DWG 75.

GROUND LINE

IGNORE RAKE
OF FORECOURT.

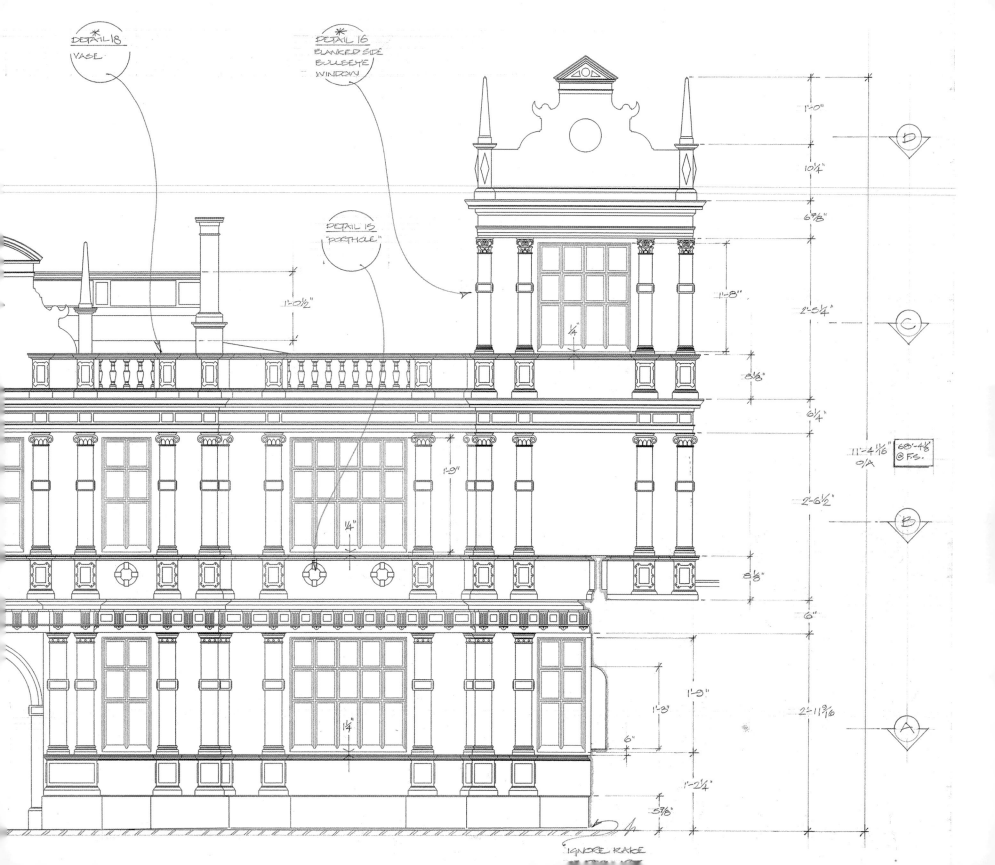

DETAIL 18
VASE

DETAIL 16
BLANKED SIDE
BULLSEYE
WINDOW

DETAIL 15
"PORTHOLE"

D

C

B

A

1'-0"

10¼"

6⅞"

2'-5¼"

1'-8"

1-0½"

8⅛"

6¼"

11'-4 11/16"
O/A

68'-4⅝"
@ F.S.

1'-9"

¼"

2'-6½"

8⅛"

6"

¼"

1'-9"

1'-3"

6"

¼"

2'-11 9/16"

1'-2¼"

5⅞"

IGNORE RAKE

JAMES GORDON

Character sketches of Detective Gordon. Simon McGuire. Digital.

LUCIUS FOX

Character sketch of Lucius Fox. Simon McGuire. Digital.

ALFRED PENNYWORTH

Character sketch of Alfred. Simon McGuire. Digital.

RACHEL DAWES

Character sketches of Rachel Dawes. Simon McGuire. Digital.

Once home, Bruce Wayne still needed time to prepare for his final transformation into Batman, and to identify his allies. Despite Gotham's decay and corruption, he could see that a few other Gothamites were holding out for truth and justice. There is, of course, faithful Alfred, who would become his right-hand man and confidant in the crusade to come. There is the middle-aged Gotham City police detective James Gordon (Gary Oldman), who wears his badge like a code of honor and refuses even a taste of the corruption practiced by his fellow cops. There is Bruce's childhood friend Rachel Dawes (Katie Holmes), keeping up the good fight as assistant district attorney. And Lucius Fox (Morgan Freeman), stuck in the Applied Science Division at Wayne Industries, would become Wayne's gatekeeper for all the prototypal military hardware a mortal crime fighter desired for arming himself for a war on evil.

Though some of the architecture and auras have been changed in *Batman Begins*, the heart of the story as Bob Kane created it is the same: Bruce Wayne embraces the darkness symbolized by the bats that frightened him as a boy when he fell down an old well into the subterranean world beneath Wayne Manor. The bats and the darkness have always been there, waiting for him, and he transforms his own fears into the symbol of his crusade, becoming a creature of the night capable of striking terror into the heart of the underworld.

Above—Bruce Wayne's supporters and accomplices. Clockwise from upper left: Detective James Gordon (Gary Oldman), Lucius Fox (Morgan Freeman), Rachel Dawes (Katie Holmes), Alfred Pennyworth (Michael Caine). David James.

Pages 110–111—A young Bruce Wayne falls down the well in his backyard, rousing the bats and unwittingly creating a future crime-fighting icon. Martin Asbury and James Cornish. Pencil and ink.

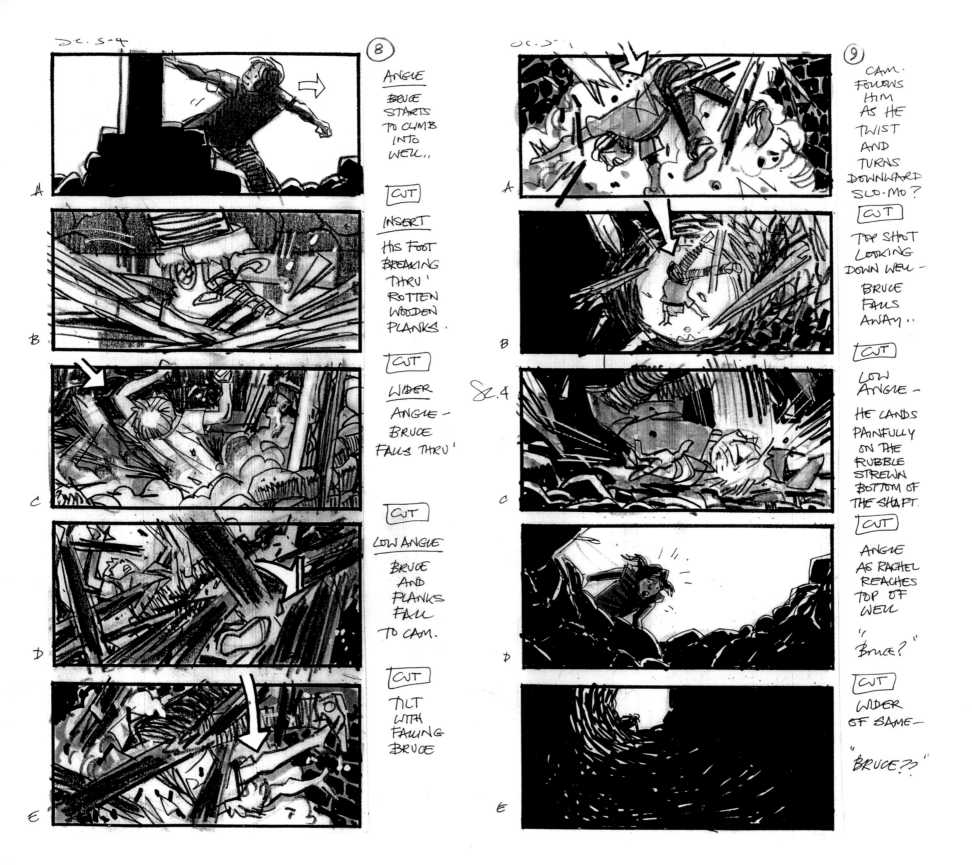

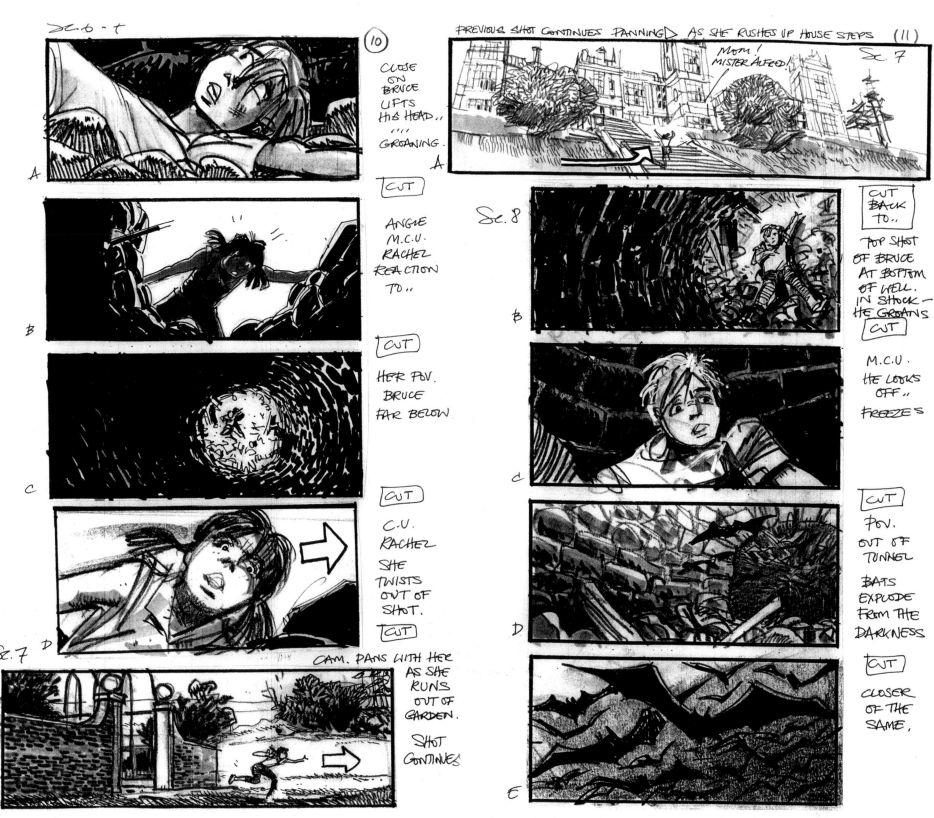

SC. 6 - 7

(10)

A — CLOSE ON BRUCE LIFTS HIS HEAD.. "" GROANING.

[CUT]

B — ANGLE M.C.U. RACHEL REACTION TO..

[CUT]

C — HER POV. BRUCE FAR BELOW.

[CUT]

D — C.U. RACHEL SHE TWISTS OUT OF SHOT.

[CUT]

Sc. 7

E — CAM. PANS WITH HER AS SHE RUNS OUT OF GARDEN. SHOT CONTINUES

PREVIOUS SHOT CONTINUES PANNING ▷ AS SHE RUSHES UP HOUSE STEPS (11)

Sc. 7

A — MOM! MISTER ALFRED!

[CUT BACK TO..]

Sc. 8

B — TOP SHOT OF BRUCE AT BOTTOM OF WELL. IN SHOCK — HE GROANS

[CUT]

C — M.C.U. HE LOOKS OFF.. FREEZES

[CUT]

D — POV. OUT OF TUNNEL BATS EXPLODE FROM THE DARKNESS

[CUT]

E — CLOSER OF THE SAME.

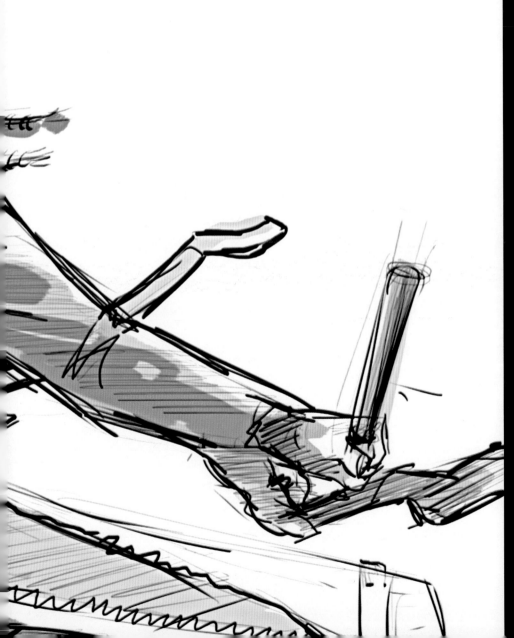

INSIDE ARKHAM

Because it was important to the filmmakers that the Batman Begins world be a closer reflection of the real world than in previous renderings—this time, nothing was to smack of "gothic"—one of the film's greatest challenges was the creation of Arkham Asylum. The asylum is one of the most gothic places in the entire Batman mythos, a gated and ghoulish nest for the criminally insane. In the echoing corridors and dungeonlike depths of Arkham, a place as irresistibly fantastic and malleable as a dream, comics creators had always let their imaginations run riot.

The production designers of Batman Begins were likewise driven by a desire to capture a feeling, not literal truth, but sustained their ties to realism by remembering that Arkham was, basically, still an institution. The team found locations in London that fit the role of a foreboding mental hospital. A chemical research lab in London's Mill Hill district served as the exterior for Arkham. For the interior, a historic but long-abandoned red-brick hotel near the King's Cross rail station in London was secured. As it had been closed for more than half a century, it offered priceless ready-made decay.

It is in Arkham Asylum that Batman encounters professor Jonathan Crane, a servant of Rā's al Ghūl. Crane's taste for terror has impelled him to invent a formula for a hallucinatory fear toxin, which Rā's al Ghūl plots to disperse throughout Gotham City by contaminating the water supply.

For his mission of terror, Crane assumes the identity of the Scarecrow, one of the lesser known but most disturbing of *Batman* comic book villains, a figure consumed by a morbid fascination with fear and a sadistic desire to trigger terror in others. Costume designer Lindy Hemming notes that some twenty major looks for the Scarecrow were explored, from a leathery gas mask to a scary skull, but they were looking too much like something lifted from an English Hammer-horror movie. "This character calls himself the Scarecrow, so we started off looking at the comics and then sculpting different [masks], but they started to look too derivative of other things," Hemming noted. "Chris and I thought that it should not be too weird, but believable."

They wanted to avoid having the Scarecrow look as if he had leapt out of the traditional, fantastical, nylon-suited super hero world. The final Scarecrow mask would have a primal feel, something a mentally disturbed person might have fashioned in a manic burst of inspiration—a burlap sack pulled over the head and tied off.

"At first, we never thought of Rā's al Ghūl and the Scarecrow in terms of a pairing," Nolan explained. "We had wanted to address the idea that Rā's al Ghūl was a mentor to Bruce Wayne; that idea had an inevitable logic that was very exciting to us. [But because Bruce breaks with Rā's], that meant that in the middle of the film, you needed someone to pick up the mantle of evil, if you like, and the Scarecrow was one of the most interesting villains, thematically. The Scarecrow uses fear as a weapon, just as Batman does. A lot of our attempts to explain why Bruce Wayne would dress up as a bat in order to fight crime had to do with exploring the symbolism and power of fear, the notion of using fear against the criminals themselves. The Scarecrow seemed a natural fit for that thematic element of the film."

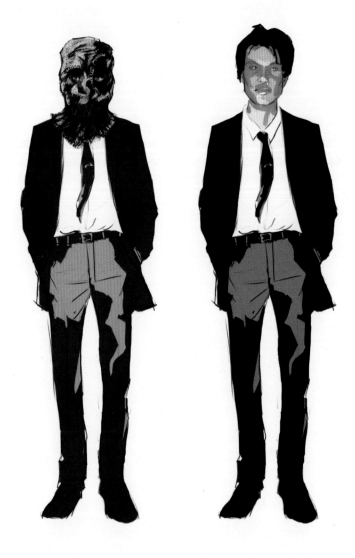

Pages 112–113—Sketch of the Scarecrow on horseback, sporting an early version of his fearful mask.
Simon McGuire. Digital.

Page 114—Arkham Asylum at night. The crew filmed exteriors at a chemical research lab in London. David James.

Page 115—Empty Arkham hallways. David James.

Above—Jonathan Crane (the Scarecrow) character sketches.
A simple burlap sack over the head transforms him into an eerily effective villain. Simon McGuire. Digital.

Opposite page—Closeup of the Scarecrow. David James.

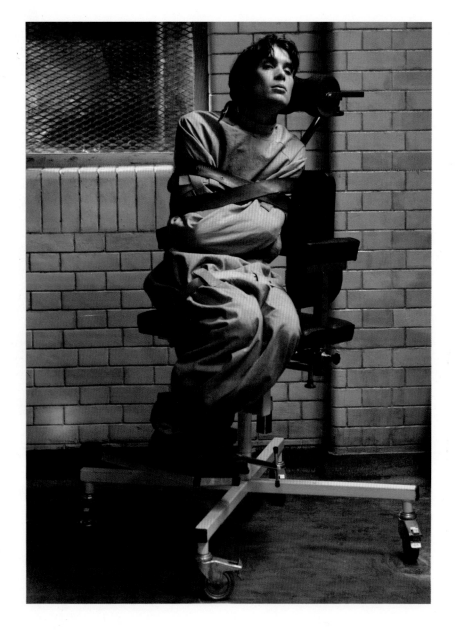

Above—Sketch of Jonathan Crane in shackles and a straightjacket. Simon McGuire. Pencil and ink.

Right—Crane's (Cillian Murphy) meek appearance belies his evil intentions. David James.

Opposite page—Crane's cell in Arkham. David James.

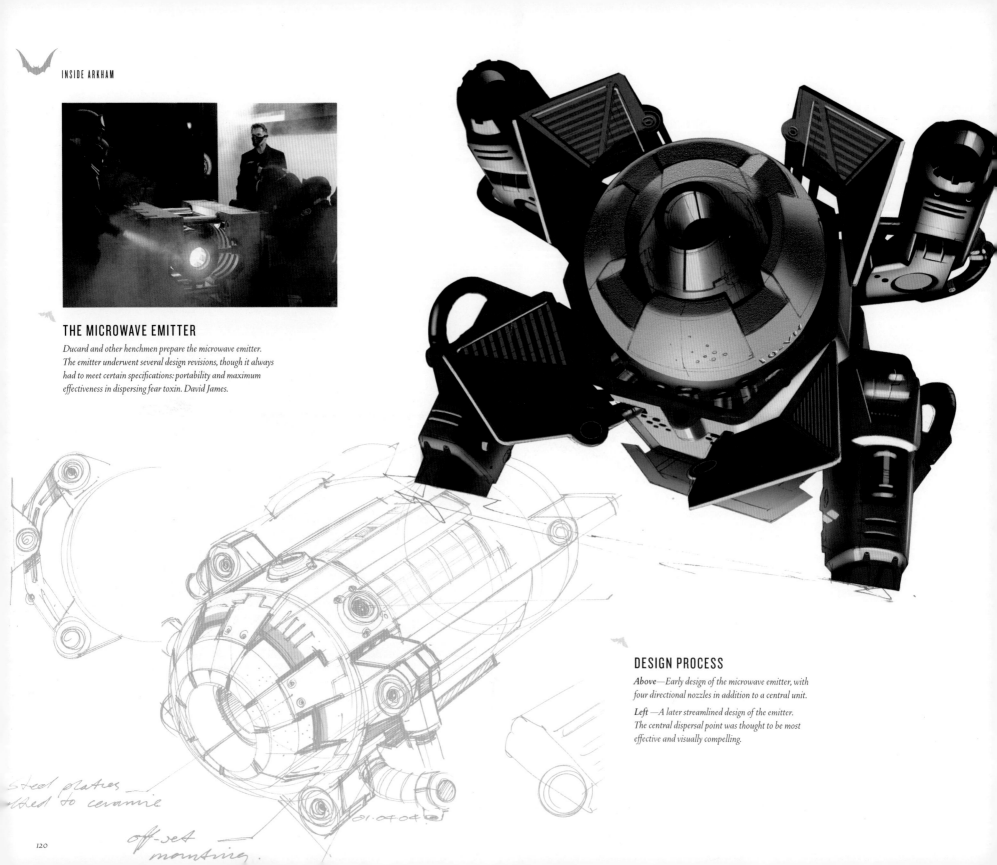

THE MICROWAVE EMITTER

*Ducard and other henchmen prepare the microwave emitter.
The emitter underwent several design revisions, though it always
had to meet certain specifications: portability and maximum
effectiveness in dispersing fear toxin. David James.*

DESIGN PROCESS

Above—Early design of the microwave emitter, with
four directional nozzles in addition to a central unit.

Left —A later streamlined design of the emitter.
The central dispersal point was thought to be most
effective and visually compelling.

steel plates
used to ceramic

off-set
mounting.

01.04.04

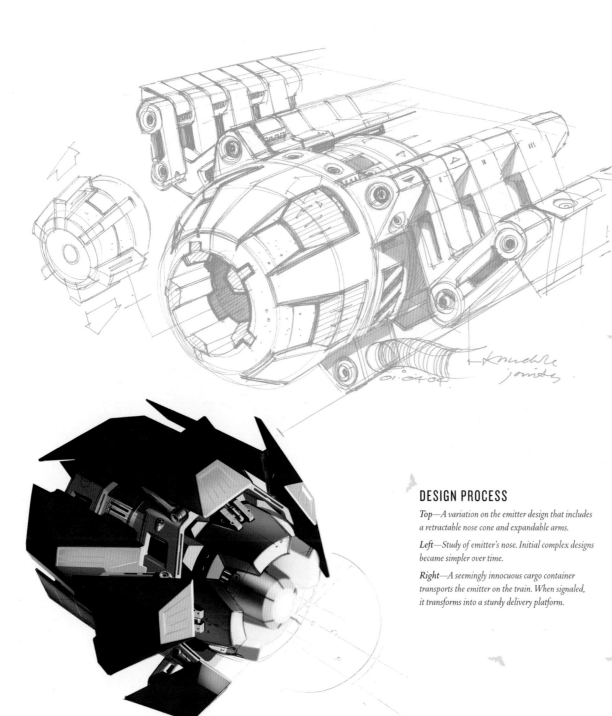

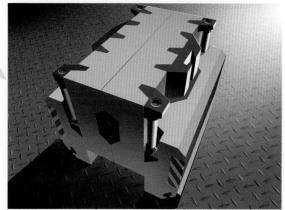

DESIGN PROCESS

Top—A variation on the emitter design that includes a retractable nose cone and expandable arms.

Left—Study of emitter's nose. Initial complex designs became simpler over time.

Right—A seemingly innocuous cargo container transports the emitter on the train. When signaled, it transforms into a sturdy delivery platform.

All illustrations by Dan Walker. Airbrush and pencil.

Batman's iconic suit received some retooling for the film as well. For the costume of his crusade, Batman would draw on the darkness of death, literally. From deep in the Applied Sciences Division, he plucked a prototype outfit once made for infantry, a Kevlar suit capable of withstanding bullets and stopping a knife. Like the Batmobile, it was fantastic, yet functional and credible. "The idea was the costume didn't need improving, it just needed representing," Nolan explained.

"One of Chris Nolan's desires was to explain where this costume comes from—most of the design work [focused on] *why* a black rubber suit," costume designer Hemming noted. "The whole idea was to make people believe that someone could make this suit."

Hemming, whose costume design credits include the last four James Bond movies, felt right at home with the notion of a high-tech "survival suit," a translucent wet suit with its inner workings visible, components designed for functions from protecting vital organs to controlling body temperature.

"Bruce Wayne takes this suit that has been made by Lucius Fox, one of the only people left at Wayne Industries who knew Thomas Wayne," Hemming explained. "Bruce Wayne takes it to his Bat-shop in his cave and begins to transform it. He paints it with the kind of black latex paint used on the Stealth bomber, which prevents the suit from having a 'heat signature' that would allow it to be tracked by infrared."

The film also gives Wayne the job of making his cowl himself, using imported material from China, with the ears rigged with built-in microphones. (The real-life designers made the cowl so that Batman could freely move his neck, unlike the solid neck piece of past Batman productions, which limited the movements of Batman actors.) The costume was completed with a pair of gauntlet-edged gloves, which the story explains were brought back by Bruce from Rā's al Ghūl's monastery.

Although the goal of the production design was to generally avoid specific

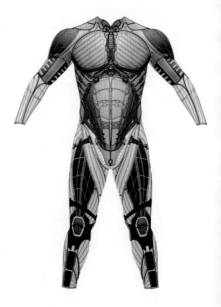

BATSUIT

The Batsuit is a fire-retardant Nomex survival suit designed by Wayne Enterprise's Applied Sciences Division for advanced infantry armed forces units. Assembled with Kevlar bi-weave fabric featuring reinforced joints, the Batsuit is tear-resistant to knife attacks and bullet resistant, repelling all ballistic projectiles except for straight-on shots at close range. Utilizing memory fabric, Batman's cape becomes rigid and conforms to predetermined shapes (glider, parachute, etc.), and allows him to stealthily swoop down upon unsuspecting opponents. Scalloped brass forearm gauntlets painted matte black can be used for climbing or to defend against a knife or sword attack.

GLOVES

Constructed of the same "memory fabric" as the rest of the Batsuit, the gloves conceal triggers that send electrical currents running through the Batsuit, causing the molecules to align and the suit to become rigid.

FOOTWEAR

Batman's boots are composed of the same material used in the Batsuit, with a hypersonic sounder concealed within the hollow heels that emits a high-frequency trill audible only to bats, causing the frenzied creatures to swarm directly to the sounder.

COWL

Another derivative of a military prototype produced by Wayne Enterprises, Batman's cowl is state-of-the-art: the graphite-composite exterior is impact-resistant, the Kevlar panel under-cowl shields Batman's head from small-caliber weapons fire, and servo-mounted high-gain stereo microphones in the ears are capable of eavesdropping on distant conversations within buildings or magnifying Batman's voice to formidable volume through a concealed loudspeaker. A radio antenna allows Batman to monitor police band and emergency response channels, nose-filters prevent toxin inhalation, Starlite night-vision lenses illuminate an adversary's every move, and hidden locking snaps prevent enemies from removing Batman's cowl and revealing his true identity should he become unconscious or incapacitated. (To avoid suspicion of his true intentions, Bruce Wayne ordered more than 10,000 cowls to be produced in Singapore, purchased via a shell corporation owned by Wayne Enterprises.)

UTILITY BELT

This streamlined belt holds everything Batman might need—a grappling gun, Mini-Mines, a cellular phone, a medi-pak, a flexible fiber-optic periscope that allows Batman to see around corners or into locked rooms, and ninja spikes (used to scale sheer walls when affixed to the hands and feet). All contents are considered nonlethal deterrents. The Utility Belt is tamper-proof, and wired with a self-destruct mechanism.

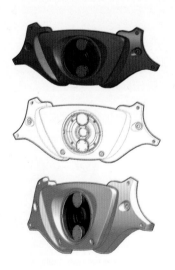

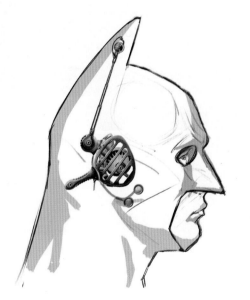

All illustrations by Simon McGuire, based on costume designs by Lindy Hemming. Digital.

"In previous film incarnations, the cape had always been, I think, something of an embarrassment, and had been minimized by making it very heavy and leathery, so it didn't flow," Nolan noted. "Yet, to us, in the comics it's always flowing and creating these great shapes."

In the story, the cape is yet another addition from the Applied Sciences Division. As Nathan Crowley noted—"we had to design this stuff to work"—so, too, did Lindy Hemming have to oversee development of a special fabric that would billow like the comics cape. In the final design the cape featured a fine nylon on the outer surface and was flocked on the underside so it could fill out with wind.

"It was very important to Chris that the cape not be stiff, that it have the floating, air-filled quality of the comics," Hemming explained. "We all wanted to cross over from those comics images and make the reason Batman looks like that *real*."

Despite the creative territory mined by others, Nolan and his production team found vast stretches of mythic terrain to explore. "There are a lot of interesting gaps, things about the origin that haven't been pinned down, which has made the Batman story more universal as a myth," Nolan mused. "That was exciting to us, that we could flesh out our own interpretation."

On all levels, *Batman Begins* was driven by the wonder of what it would be like if Batman actually existed. And so the filmmakers dreamed, and conjured Batman's world anew—a reflection of our world. And they traveled to the heart of an elemental myth, defining the dimensions of a dark resurrection. Bruce Wayne was almost consumed by the darkness—he knows the evil that men do, how they feed on the blood of innocents. But he emerged from that darkness on the wings of a night creature: reborn, the origin story proclaims, as "this avenger of evil, The BATMAN."

Opposite page—Concept illustration of a flowing cape. The Batman Begins *Batsuit employs a fluid and cinematic design. Simon McGuire, based on costume designs by Lindy Hemming. Digital.*

Top left—Batman's sophisticated cape can become a rigid set of wings, allowing silent flight and the element of surprise. David James.

Left—Highly theatrical and deceptive, the Batsuit is designed to strike fear into the hearts of criminals. David James.

Pages 130–131—Storyboards of Batman crashing in on Falcone. Wayne is using his Batsuit to good effect, inspiring fear by dropping in unannounced. Martin Asbury and James Cornish. Pencil and ink.

Page 132—Batman pauses next to the Batmobile in the Batcave. David James.

Page 133—Close-up of the Caped Crusader. David James.

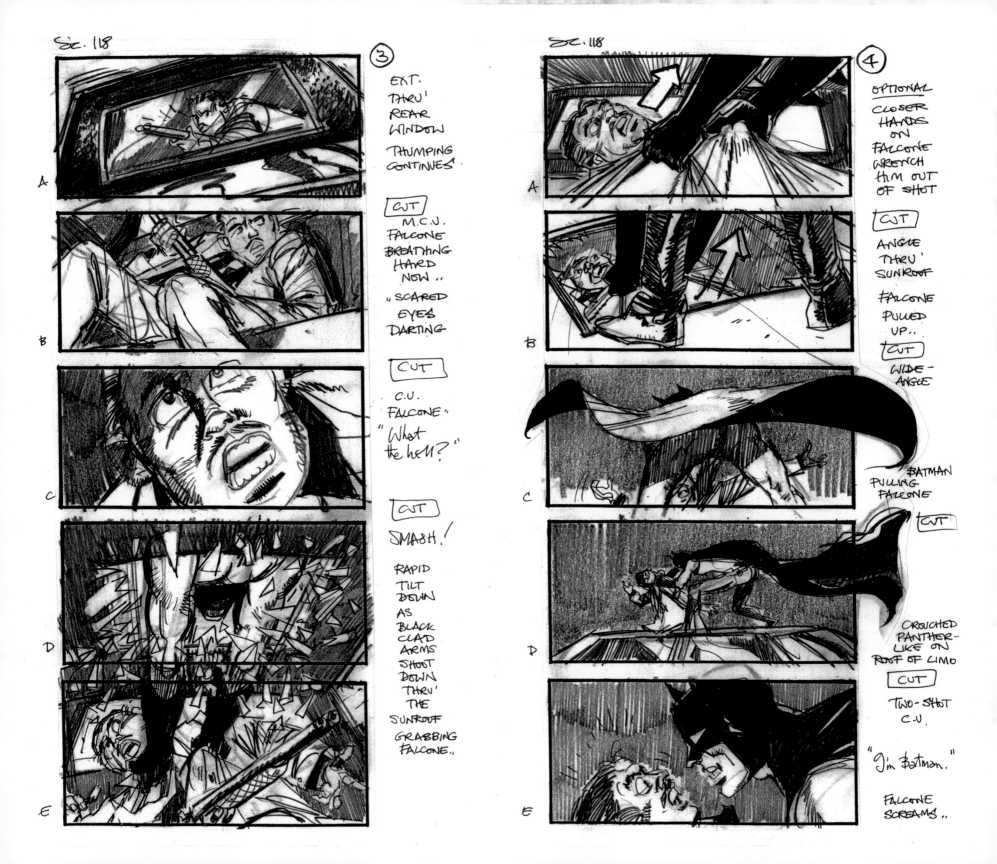

A

EXT.
THRU'
REAR
WINDOW

THUMPING
CONTINUES.

CUT
M.C.U.
FALCONE
BREATHING
HARD
NOW ..

"SCARED
EYES
DARTING

B

CUT

C.U.
FALCONE.

"What
the hell?"

C

CUT

SMASH!

RAPID
TILT
DOWN
AS
BLACK
CLAD
ARMS
SHOOT
DOWN
THRU'
THE
SUNROOF
GRABBING
FALCONE..

D

E

OPTIONAL
CLOSER
HANDS
ON
FALCONE
WRENCH
HIM OUT
OF SHOT

A

CUT
ANGLE
THRU'
SUNROOF

FALCONE
PULLED
UP..

CUT

B

WIDE-
ANGLE

BATMAN
PULLING
FALCONE

C

CUT

CROUCHED
PANTHER-
LIKE ON
ROOF OF LIMO

D

CUT
TWO-SHOT
C.U.

"I'm Batman."

FALCONE
SCREAMS ..

E

Sc. 119 — 5

A — EXT. THE SCREAM ECHOES DOWN THE ALLEY.

HOMELESS MAN LOOKS UP FROM HIS BRAZIER

CUT

B — CLOSER — HE PEERS DOWN ALLEY

SEEING BATMAN ON CAR ROOF —

ICONIC, CLOAK BILLOWING

C — CLOSER OF SAME

CUT

D — CLOSER STILL TO..,

E — C.U. BATMAN TO CAM. "Nice coat."

Sc. 119 — 6

A — BATMAN FLIES UP FROM THE LIMO

CUT

B — WIDER — RAPID TILT

CUT

C — C.U. HOMELESS MAN GOBSMACKED "...Thanks..."

CUT

D — HIS POV. NOTHING ABOVE.. BATMAN HAS VANISHED.

GRAPPLING GUN

The pneumatic grappling gun features a magnetic grapple and monofilament de-cel climbing line tested to 350 pounds maximum holding strength. Early renditions borrowed from centuries-old musket design, as well as modern firearms. The final version, in keeping with the design of much of the film, is streamlined, simple, and extremely effective.

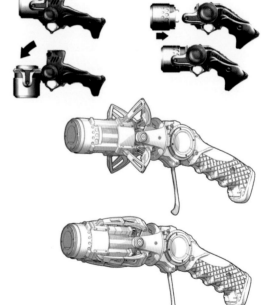

MINI-MINES

Mini-Mines and explosives packets can be used for a variety of offensive and defensive purposes, including creating diversions, disabling getaway vehicles, or defeating locks.

INJECTOR

Designed to deliver the antidote to the Scarecrow's fear gas, the injector is another Wayne Enterprises product that shrank to a more manageable size in the final film.

All illustrations by Simon McGuire. Digital.

Concept art of the corrupt Falcone bound and splayed across a spotlight, creating an impromptu Bat-Signal.
Simon McGuire, based on costume design by Lindy Hemming. Digital.

ACKNOWLEDGMENTS

My thanks to Sarah Malarkey at Chronicle Books and Steve Korté at DC Comics for giving me a round-trip ticket to Gotham City (although, once you've been to Gotham you never really leave). I also appreciate the efforts of Susannah Scott and Irika Slavin at Warner Bros., who helped with numerous logistical matters. And a big Batman thank-you to Emma Thomas, Shane Thompson, and the Batman Begins *team in London.*

I'm appreciative of the kind turns and help of Matt Robinson at Chronicle and Chris Cerasi at DC. A bow and best regards to Kevin Bricklin at Warner Bros. Worldwide Publishing and Charles Kochman at DC Licensed Publications for giving me a lift early on, when I was out on the road and hitchhiking to Gotham.

Finally, I'm thankful for the wonderful insights and good humor of Nathan Crowley, who literally took me to where Batman Begins *began—the garage at the Nolan home. I also appreciate Chris Nolan having taken time from his all-consuming* Batman *editorial demands to share his thoughts about the making of this movie. Thank you, Chris.*

—Mark Cotta Vaz

A windblown Batman surveys Gotham from a rooftop exhaust vent. Dermot Power. Digital.

Opposite page—Concept art based on image by Jim Lee and Scott Williams from Batman *#614 (June 2003).*
Nathan Crowley. Digital.

Pages 142–143—Christian Bale as the Batman steps behind the camera. David James.

Page 144—Motion study of Batman in a vertical climb, aided by his pneumatic grappling gun. Simon McGuire. Digital.